MW00807442

GHOSTS
OF THE
QUAD CITIES

MICHAEL McCARTY AND MARK McLAUGHLIN
INTRODUCTION BY THE AMAZING KRESKIN

Haunted
America

Published by Haunted America
A Division of The History Press
Charleston, SC
www.historypress.com

Copyright © 2019 by Michael McCarty and Mark McLaughlin
All rights reserved

First published 2019

Manufactured in the United States

ISBN 9781467141062

Library of Congress Control Number: 2019943508

Notice: The information in this book is true and complete to the best of our knowledge. It is offered without guarantee on the part of the authors or The History Press. The authors and The History Press disclaim all liability in connection with the use of this book.

All rights reserved. No part of this book may be reproduced or transmitted in any form whatsoever without prior written permission from the publisher except in the case of brief quotations embodied in critical articles and reviews.

CONTENTS

Contents

Acknowledgements

Michael McCarty

My lovely wife, Cindy McCarty; my collaborator and good friend Mark McLaughlin; The Amazing Kreskin; Latte the Bunny; Chef Steph; Jack, Colleen, Camilla, Holly, Bruce, Ray, Jo Ann and Jimmy Brown; Carma and Roy; Cathy and Steve; Brian and Quinn and Izzy; Scott Faust; Ron Stewart; Igor's Bistro; and the memory of my parents, Bev and Gerald McCarty.

Mark McLaughlin

My amazing friend and frequent collaborator Michael Sheehan Jr., Annikin the Super-Cat, Michael McCarty (who's also a great friend and collaborator!), Cindy and Latte, my dear sister-from-another-mister Martha G.T., Karen B., Pam M., Jan D., Denise A., Jake E. and Paula S., Quinn H., Brian K. and Mary B.G. Also, a big *thank-you* to the authors who have inspired me: H.P. Lovecraft, Robert Aickman, Robert Bloch, Bram Stoker and Mary Wollstonecraft Shelley.

BOTH MARK AND MIKE

The Amazing Kreskin, Haunted America, The History Press, Chad Rhoad, Kyle Dickson, the German American Heritage Center, The Source Bookstore, The Book Rack, Barnes & Noble, Don D'Ammassa, the Darker Side of Davenport tours, Ray Congrove, Bruce Walters, John Brassard Jr., Cassie Steffen, the Broadway Paranormal Society, Ariel Young, Rock Island Paranormal, Joyce Godwin Grubbs, the Quad Cities Convention & Visitors Bureau, the Midwest Writing Center, Mel Piff, Augustana College, St. Ambrose University, Palmer College of Chiropractics, Scott Community College, Joan Mauch, Jonathan Turner, John Marx, Rick Lopez, Igor's Bistro, Richard-Sloane Special Collection of the Davenport Public Library, Jeff Ernst, Kai Swanson, Stephanie Smith, Bill Michaels, Greg Dwyer, *The Dwyer & Michaels Show*, Doug Miller, Kyle Carter, the *Quad-City Times*, the *Rock Island Argus*, the *Moline Dispatch*, *Paula Sands Live*, City of Rock Island, Jill Doak, Miles Brainard, Downtown Davenport Partnership, Quad Cities Chamber of Commerce and the Quad Cities for being so supportive of our work, and, of course, Benjamin Gibson, our fearless editor, who guided us through the winding course of getting this book published.

INTRODUCTION

BY THE AMAZING KRESKIN

It's with much pride and joy that I introduce you to Michael McCarty and Mark McLaughlin's new work, *Ghosts of the Quad Cities*. Mike and Mark have put together what I can predict is going to be a remarkable reading experience that will mesmerize your interest and attention.

To take an area of the country with much history—where thousands of people have lived and died—and to uncover mysterious and unexplainable phenomena is to me one of the most ingenious and refreshing investigations of a historic nature. You just can't walk into a library today and pull out history books that are going to also take you to a time and period where unexplainable phenomena are taking place.

I can assure you that McCarty and McLaughlin have created a riveting work. I dare not overlook sharing the fact with you that Mike played a major role in my career by coauthoring my book, *Conversations with Kreskin*, but we go back further—and ironically, find ourselves in the Quad Cities.

It was the beginning of a tour in May 1991, in the state of Iowa. I was opening in a comedy club in Davenport that evening. I had done many university performances in the United States, so there was great interest in my work among students.

I came over to the frat house Phi Kappa Chi at Palmer College in Davenport, Iowa. Mike McCarty helped immensely by finding the location and putting everything together. He could not have picked a better setting. It presented an amazing opportunity for young people to be awakened to unique, memorable experiences.

The Amazing Kreskin has mystified and entertained millions all over the world with his live two-hour one-man show. Kreskin has also starred in his own TV show, *The Amazing World of Kreskin*; has record-setting hundreds of television appearances on shows hosted by Joey Bishop, Mike Douglas, Steve Allen, Johnny Carson (even inspired Carson's skit "The Great Carnac"), Dinah Shore, Phil Donahue, Larry King, Howard Stern and Jimmy Fallon and on CNN, Fox, CBS, ABC and NBC; and he is the author of over twenty bestselling books about the mind, his abilities and his career. *Courtesy of The Amazing Kreskin.*

Michael had first met me when he was working at the Funny Bone Comedy Club in Davenport. At that time, Mike was a promotion coordinator, and he was truly instrumental in finding a location for a séance that I wanted to do for the press. Mike managed to pull all of this together, and the media response was remarkable.

Coverage included a local television station, news crews and newspaper people. There were even disc jockeys who attended the séance. What was exciting for the Phi Kappa Chi students was to have them attend the séance, sitting around the large table where the event would take place. Quite a number of people wanted to participate in the experience, but I narrowed it down to thirteen and we went downstairs, where the press could cover the scenario.

To tap into whatever happenings may be available in the room and setting, I spelled my name a number of times. During this time, people had formed a circle with hands on each other's shoulders, and after I spelled my name, I instructed them to drop their arms. One of the people involved experienced considerable analgesia, and one boy's arms twisted almost out of shape, like someone was holding or twisting his arm. They felt the floor literally vibrating, with a heavy chill going through the room.

The media's response was very positive and exciting. It was clear to all of them that this was not some group of actors or play performers. These people were actually responding to some kind of force or phenomenon and couldn't quite explain what or how it was happening. Whether I had awakened some unique force or potential within those participating, or had made them aware and sensitive to phenomena existing within the room or setting, there was no question that a force of reality was taking place and being experienced by all of them.

Let me introduce to you another unusual experience that occurred while I was investigating a haunted house. It was all the more unusual because no one could have predicted how this investigation would have ended and why it ended the way it did.

I have visited many homes and dwellings around the world that were supposed to be haunted, and I've said on a number of occasions that there are certain rooms and buildings I've entered that seem to have a "spirit" or climate all their own.

Years ago in Nyack, New York, I flew out to investigate a home that was thought to be haunted. As I walked through the building, I was able to describe the areas of the house where the owners had apparently seen a ghost or spirit, and it became a subject for discussion. The follow-up is fascinating.

They put the house up for sale, and I had thought of possibly purchasing it but didn't really want to move to that part of New York. Incidentally, the house was only a few buildings away from Helen Hayes's home in the same area.

We decided to have a séance in the house. Howard Stern was going to cover it live on the radio. It would have provided tremendous publicity for the family who wanted to sell their home. Just a few days before the scheduled séance, a member of the family let us know that each reporter coming to the home would have to pay a sum. To be honest with you, I don't recall if it was $50, $75 or what have you. Well, that ended it. I canceled my plans, Stern wouldn't think of stepping into such a setting, and there was no séance. The publicity that could have been bought for thousands of dollars never took place. Bear in mind I had already done many TV shows promoting the house, and in a number of them, the mother had joined me on camera.

They finally sold the home. But, within a year or so the buyers demanded that the previous owners, who had moved to Florida and retired, take the house back. The buyers had encountered uncomfortable experiences in the home, as if it were haunted. Don't you know, the owner had never told them that there were haunting incidents within the home. The courts ruled that they had to give the money back and accept the return of the house—which they inevitably sold again for a lesser price.

Each séance is a different experience, a different adventure—even in the case of the Nyack home, in which the séance never came to be!

Well folks, I see the curtains are beginning to part and the full spotlight is filling the stage with color and mystery. Please join these two fabulous and mysterious authors on a spectral adventure in the haunted Midwest!

ABOUT THE QUAD CITIES

The Iowa/Illinois Quad Cities is an urban area composed of five cities: Davenport and Bettendorf on the Iowa side of the Mississippi River and Rock Island, Moline and East Moline on the Illinois side. There are also many smaller communities surrounding the five major ones.

For years, Quad-Citians—or Quad-Citizens, as they have been called in recent years—have mulled over the question: If we live in the Quad Cities, why is the area composed of five major cities?

Back in the 1940s, the area used to be called the Tri-Cities, after Davenport, Rock Island and Moline. But then the neighboring communities of Bettendorf and East Moline began to grow. The name Quad Cities soon came into favor, while Quint Cities never built up enough steam to catch on. Maybe someday!

The name Quad Cities is reinforced by the fact that the cities span four counties: Scott County in Iowa and Henry, Mercer and Rock Island in Illinois. Thanks to a bend in the Mississippi, the river flows from east to west through the area.

A QUAD CITIES OVERVIEW

Davenport, the largest community in the Quad Cities, was established in 1836. In 2016, Davenport had a reported population of 102,612.

Moline was platted in 1843 under the name of Rock Island Mills. It was changed to Moline in 1848. In 2010, it had a reported population of 43,977.

Rock Island was platted in 1835 under the name of Stephenson. The name was changed to Rock Island in 1841. In 2000, the city's population was 39,684.

Bettendorf was established in 1903. Bettendorf's population was 33,217 in the 2010 census.

East Moline was established in 1903, and its population was 21,302 in the 2010 census.

BUSINESSES OF THE QUAD CITIES

Some of the largest employers in the Quad Cities include the Rock Island Arsenal, Deere & Company, Genesis Health System, Hy-Vee, UnityPoint Health, Arconic (formerly Alcoa), Tyson Fresh Meats, Oscar Mayer/Kraft, Isle Casino Hotel and Tri-City Electric Company.

A HISTORY OF THE QUAD CITIES: BEFORE THE CITIES WERE BUILT

We include elements from the history of the Quad Cities in many of the chapters in this book. Here is a quick overview of the area's history *before* the cities were built.

The people of the Woodland tribes were the first to inhabit the area now known as the Quad Cities. Their burial mounds, which can still be found today, date back to 200 BC. After the Woodlands came the Sauk and Fox Indians. A Sauk village was located where the Rock River empties into the mighty Mississippi River. This was the largest Indian settlement in North America, with a population somewhere between six and seven thousand.

The Fox Indian tribe, also known as the Mesquakie, settled near the Sauks and created more villages up and down the Mississippi River. One of those villages is now the location of downtown Rock Island.

The lives of the Indians changed considerably once the European influence entered the area. The Indians traded with the French, were allies with the British and often wore western clothing. They hunted with rifles and lived in wooden structures. But the Indians' dealings with the newcomers to their regions weren't always agreeable. In 1831, Native Americans on the Illinois side were forced to move across the river to Iowa after a series of treaties and land cessions. In this instance, a cession is the act of giving up land as part of an agreement in a treaty.

In 1832, Sauk warrior Black Hawk refused to accept the treaty and allow his people's Illinois land to be taken from them. So, he led more than 1,500 followers back across the Mississippi River to reclaim their territory. However, the revolt, which came to be known as the Black Hawk War, was quickly defeated. An interesting historical note: Black Hawk was one of two Native Americans in American history with a war named after him. The other was Metacomet, a Wampanoag chief who adopted the name Philip, after whom King Philip's War was named.

The land originally owned by the Native Americans was acquired by treaty following their defeat by the United States. The cession of six million acres of Iowa land was known as the Black Hawk Purchase. The purchase was made for $640,000 on September 21, 1832.

Thanks to Black Hawk's bravery and determination, he became a local and national hero. The Black Hawk State Historical Site in Rock Island rests on the former Sauk village area and is now a museum dedicated to preserving the history of the Indian warrior and the Sauk people.

"After the Blackhawk Purchase of 1832, settlement of eastern Iowa was opened up the next year," said John Brassard Jr., author of *Murder & Mayhem in Scott County, Iowa* and coauthor of the book *Scott County Cemeteries*. Brassard added:

> Antoine LeClaire, who served as the translator at the purchase, received large tracts of land from grateful members of the Sauk tribe. With this land, he and others founded the city of Davenport, named after Col. George Davenport, a successful fur trader. Other towns cropped up throughout Scott County, newly formed in 1837. Over the next several decades, Davenport and these other towns throughout the county grew and gave rise to successful, interesting citizens of their own. Some were inventors like William Bettendorf, who created the Bettendorf Truck.

QUAD CITIES IN THE ENTERTAINMENT INDUSTRY

The Quad Cities may not be a showbiz mecca like Hollywood, but the area has been featured in plenty of movies and TV programs over the years.

The Blues Brothers mentioned Rock Island in their first album, *Briefcase Full of Blues*—"from Rock Island, Illinois, the blues of 'Joliet' Jake and Elwood Blues, The Blues Brothers."

The original plot of the 1980 movie *The Blues Brothers* and in the liner notes of *Briefcase Full of Blues* revealed that the brothers grew up in an orphanage in Rock Island. But director John Landis's request to film in the area was denied because it would portray the community as a "rowdy blues city."

About five years later, the Quad Cities Blues Fest was held for the first time. This annual event is held on the banks of the Mississippi River in downtown Davenport. About two decades later, Rock Island would commemorate the Blues Brothers with a statue in the city's downtown area, which is a fun locale for Quad-Citians who enjoy the nightlife.

Rock Island was the setting of the movie *The Road to Perdition*. See the John Looney and Rock Island Arsenal chapters in this book for more details.

The area was also mentioned at the beginning of the movie *Nothing in Common*, starring Tom Hanks and Jackie Gleason. Hanks asked another character, who was from the Quad Cities, if it was twice as good as the Twin Cities. Also, David Spade asked for directions on how to find Davenport in the movie *Tommy Boy*.

Many movies were shot in the Quad Cities, including the campy 1991 horror-comedy *Beauty Queen Butcher*. "Both myself and comedian and actor Jason Stuart auditioned for that movie," said author Michael McCarty, "and neither one of us got a part. You can say, I didn't make the 'cut,' I know, it is a bad pun. But hey, no one said showbiz was easy!"

Bix, an Interpretation of a Legend (also known as *Bix, une interprétation de la légende*) is a 1991 Italian dramatic film about the final years of cornet player and jazz legend Bix Beiderbecke. Bix was born in Davenport, so the movie was shot there. It was directed by Pupi Avati. Author Mark McLaughlin auditioned for the movie and was cast as an extra. "I can be seen for a few seconds, clapping in a speakeasy scene," McLaughlin said. "Also, at one point, you can see me walking briskly across a ballroom. Don't blink or you'll miss me entirely." See the Oakdale Cemetery chapter for more details about Bix.

The 1994 Italian TV movie *An American Love*, starring Brooke Shields, was shot in the Quad Cities, and the performers took in the sights while they were in town. "Both Brooke Shields and Woody Harrelson stopped by to catch a show at the Funny Bone Comedy Club back when I worked there," said McCarty.

The Hideout (also known as *Il nascondiglio*) is a 2007 Italian suspense film directed by Pupi Avati. It was shot in the Quad Cities, and McLaughlin also auditioned for this one. "My role in this one was a little bigger than my part in *Bix*," he said. "I played a male nurse who loaded a suitcase into a shuttle."

Sugar, a critically acclaimed 2008 film about a teenager from the Dominican Republic who comes to America, was shot primarily at Modern Woodmen Park in Davenport.

The 2009 SyFy channel movie *Megafault* and a *Children of the Corn* remake, also released in 2009, were both shot in the Quad Cities.

FINAL WORDS ABOUT THE QUAD CITIES

Towns and cities have thrived in this area for more than 180 years. That's not even counting the Native Americans who lived in the area for centuries before that.

Consider the many generations, the many thousands of lives spent in the Quad Cities area. With so many lives over so many years, it can't be helped that there would be a plethora of departed souls. In this book, we will examine ghostly manifestations that have been reported in the Quad Cities over the years.

So, sit back and enjoy these hauntings with an open mind. Try not to be doubtful! After all…do any of us really know if the souls of the deceased can linger after death? Unless you've already had your funeral, there's no way you can really say for sure!

WHAT DOES *HAUNTED* MEAN?

When most people think of hauntings, their thoughts usually connect with memories of movies they've seen. Certainly, over the decades, ghost movies have evolved substantially. Older films, particularly those from the black-and-white era, tended to depict ghosts as spooky spectral creatures, more stylish than ghoulish. Many times, the ghosts were simply characters portrayed in a semi-transparent manner—as if to say, "Look, they're not even solid. Nothing to be afraid of here."

Sometimes the ghosts turned out to be real people masquerading as ghosts. For example, the 1939 movie *The Cat and the Canary* tells of a house infested with macabre spirits and a homicidal maniac, but really, the only evil presence is a regular human being in a cheap mask. Also, think of all those *Scooby-Doo, Where Are You!* episodes where the "ghost" turned out to be a crooked individual pretending to be a supernatural presence so that folks would stay away from a particular building or area.

As horror films became more visceral, their ghosts also became more substantial and monstrous. The supernatural creatures in the 1982 film *Poltergeist* were more demonic and clearly supernatural. The year before, the movie *The Evil Dead* brought trans-dimensional, hellish horrors into the mix. The movie was clearly inspired by the monster-heavy fiction of H.P. Lovecraft. In fact, *The Evil Dead* even features the *Necronomicon*, a fictional book of sorcery that was an essential part of the fiction of Lovecraft.

None of the Midwest hauntings covered by this book include trans-dimensional gateways, exorcists, ravenous ghouls or tentacled monsters. You won't find any crooks in rubber masks, either. Those are all characters and creatures from horror movies.

Outside of movies, in real life, one is more likely to find that hauntings are more subtle. But that doesn't mean those hauntings are less credible. Thinking that reality should emulate Hollywood special effects is a lot to ask!

As you read about these many hauntings in the Midwest, remember: the majority of them are subtle, but maybe that's the way the paranormal usually manifests itself.

As a shadow, not a monster.

As a whisper, not a scream.

DAVENPORT, IOWA

Hotel Blackhawk

T he Hotel Blackhawk, located at 200 East Third Street in downtown Davenport, is an eleven-story building over 140 feet tall. This brick and terra-cotta building is connected to a convention center known as the RiverCenter by a sky bridge, and it is also adjacent to the Adler Theatre. It is a Marriott Autograph Collection property and a member of Historic Hotels of America. It has been listed in the National Register of Historic Places since 1983.

Built and developed by Davenport businessman W.F. Miller, the Hotel Blackhawk first opened its doors for business on February 16, 1915. "The United States of America experienced an economic boom in the Roaring Twenties, but Davenport had it before then," said Kyle Dickson, assistant director of the German American Heritage Center.

"It has a real nice ballroom and of course, many famous people have stayed at the Hotel Blackhawk," Dickson said. "Guests have included writer Carl Sandburg, actor Cary Grant, and President Richard Nixon." The hotel has named rooms 412–14 the Nixon Suite.

Other luminaries who have stayed in the hotel include President Barack Obama, Vice President Walter Mondale, gangster Al Capone, baseball legend Babe Ruth, singer Tony Bennett and comedians Milton Berle and Red Skelton. The big bands led by Guy Lombardo and Stan Kenton have performed there, as well as Pearl Bailey and Bix Beiderbecke. President Ronald Reagan held a campaign stop there as well.

The Hotel Blackhawk, located at 200 East Third Street, downtown Davenport, Iowa, is an eleven-story building, over 140 feet tall. This brick and terra-cotta structure is connected by a sky bridge to a convention center known as the RiverCenter. It is also adjacent to the Adler Theatre. It is a Marriott Autograph Collection property and a member of Historic Hotels of America. It has been listed in the National Register of Historic Places since 1983. *Photo by Michael McCarty.*

THE GHOST OF CARY GRANT

On November 29, 1986, actor Cary Grant died following a brief stay in the hotel. His room was on the eighth floor, and he was going to perform that night in *A Conversation with Cary Grant* at the Adler Theatre next door. Sadly, Grant passed away before his appearance. He experienced a massive stroke and was taken to St. Luke's Hospital on Kimberly Road, where he passed away at age eighty-two.

Cary Grant was born Archibald Alec Leach on January 18, 1904, in the Bristol, England suburb of Horfield. Known for his sophisticated accent and suave demeanor, he was considered to be one of Hollywood's classic leading men. In 1999, the American Film Institute proclaimed Cary Grant to be the second-greatest male film star of Golden Age Hollywood—Humphrey Bogart being No. 1.

When Cary Grant died, *People* magazine wrote, in an article about the actor, "How unfortunate Grant died in such an unglamorous berg as Davenport, Iowa." That line set off a firestorm of protest from thousands of people in the Quad Cities area, including angry letters to the editor, comments on television and radio and banning of the publication from several newsstands in the region.

Money talks, and the editors must have listened. *People* soon retracted the comment, and the magazine went back on the newsstands in the area.

Though Grant did not die in the hotel, it was the location of the stroke that led to his demise. So perhaps his spirit might have been bound to the hotel in some profound way. Many people have said that they've spotted Grant's ghost in the hotel over the years. "Most of the stories come from people seeing an elderly gentleman in the lobbies," Dickson said. "Many claim it is Cary Grant, an elderly, well-dressed gentleman. That is what everyone has said."

During the 1970s, the hotel fell on hard times. Plans were considered to convert the hotel into a three-hundred-unit elderly care faculty. Thankfully, the fulfillment of those plans did not become necessary.

In time, the St. Louis–based firm Restoration St. Louis launched more than $40 million in renovations to the hotel. The improvements were carried out from April 2009 to December 2010. "Ever since Restoration St. Louis has brought the Hotel Blackhawk back to its glamour, people have been noticing more ghosts," Dickson said.

Another ghost seen frequently is a woman floating down the hallways to the grand ballroom. "She's in an evening gown, so she looks like she's dressed up," he said. "That's what people say."

He noted that the Whistler is another ghost that has been seen—but more often heard—at the hotel. "Basically, he whistles really loud to get your attention and slips behind a corner, so you might not see him," Dickson said. "You can always hear him, but you can barely get a glimpse of him, sneaking behind the corner before you get him."

Dickson also mentioned that in the ballroom, the piano has been heard to play by itself. "People will hear the sounds of a piano, but that is generally it," he said.

Happily, the ghosts people have noticed are all of the harmless variety—including the elegant celebrity ghost of Cary Grant.

Oakdale Cemetery

The Oakdale Memorial Gardens, formerly known as Oakdale Cemetery, is located at 2501 Eastern Avenue in Davenport, Iowa. It was established as a nonprofit cemetery by a group of businessmen as an alternative to the for-profit Pine Hill Cemetery, and they thought that City of Davenport Cemetery didn't have enough room to accommodate the expanding city. The City Cemetery wasn't overcrowded at that point, but the group figured that it might be one day in the future.

It was incorporated as the Oakdale Cemetery Company on May 14, 1856, according to the Oakdale website (http://www.oakdalememorialgardens. org/history.html). It is a peaceful, beautiful locale, and Oakdale Memorial Gardens even has a section for the burial of pets called Love of Animals Petland.

The cemetery has graves dating back to the Victorian era, and many famous and influential Quad-Citians sleep forever in its tranquil grounds. One such prominent individual is legendary jazz artist Leon Bismark "Bix" Beiderbecke. The renowned cornet player's grave receives thousands of visitors each year. Incidentally, Bix's brother, Charles Beiderbecke, was Oakdale's sexton at one time.

A *Quad-City Times* article, "The Bleak Cemetery of Forgotten Children" by Bill Wundram, states that 257 orphans from the Civil War era are buried at Oakdale. According to the article, they were the children of men killed in the war, with no place to put them. Annie Wittenmyer, a nurse/hero, lobbied for "an orphan asylum" to be built in Davenport.

Oakdale Cemetery, where Leon "Bix" Beiderbecke is buried. The tradition of leaving coins on a headstone lets the family of the deceased know that you paid respects. *Photo by Michael McCarty.*

Born in Ohio, Sarah "Annie" Turner Wittenmyer (1827–1900) was a writer, social reformer and humanitarian. Committed to serving the community, she was the first president of the Woman's Christian Temperance Union. She was instrumental in establishing the Iowa Soldiers' Orphans' Home, which was renamed the Annie Wittenmyer Home in 1949.

Wittenmyer made it her mission to help children throughout her life. She even established a Sunday school and a tuition-free school for underprivileged young people. Tragically, fate did not reward her well for all that she did for children. Of her own four children, only one lived to reach adulthood.

It is said that the Annie Wittenmyer section of Oakdale is the final resting place of children who died in a fire at the orphanage that Wittenmyer championed. Plus, rumor has it that at times, you can hear the ghost-children screaming for help.

According to John Brassard Jr., coauthor of the book *Scott County Cemeteries*, it is said that a lot of orphans from Annie Wittenmyer's orphanage were buried at the cemetery. "A big fire took place at Annie Wittenmyer and a bunch of orphans died and they were buried at that section at Oakdale," he said. "If you go there, you can hear little kids screaming and crying."

But, Brassard went on to add, "According to 'The Orphans of Oakdale Cemetery,' an October 13, 2008 blog post published by the Richard-Sloane Special Collection of the Davenport Public Library, there were three fires that took place at Annie Wittenmyer, but there were no casualties. There was a lot of property damage, thousands of dollars' worth of damage, but no casualties. Most of the kids who were buried there were because of an illness of some kind—infections, diphtheria, typhoid, anything like that.

"But no fire.

Oakdale Cemetery is located at 2501 Eastern Avenue, Davenport. This is the front entrance to the graveyard. *Photo by Michael McCarty.*

"Also, if you've ever been out to Oakdale and have spent any time out there, you'll see it's surrounded by residential neighborhoods. If you hear a little kid crying or screaming, it could just be little kids playing. It could be a kid being yelled at by his mom. You can easily pawn it off," commented John Brassard Jr.

Over the years, paranormal activities have been reported in Oakdale Memorial Gardens. It is said that if you take photographs of the cemetery, mist and orbs will appear in the photos. Also, there have been sightings of a shadow person darting back and forth between the tombstones and the trees at dusk.

The question is, are these actual manifestations of the paranormal or the results of overactive imaginations? The thought of death can summon a variety of emotions, so the sights and sounds of a cemetery can do much to fuel the imaginations of receptive minds. As Brassard noted, the sound of children playing in the distance can easily be misinterpreted as the screams of ghost-children.

But then, maybe it *takes* a receptive mind to be able to observe the paranormal. Obviously, ghosts do not reveal themselves to everyone. After all, if ghosts *did* make their presence known to one and all on a regular basis, the existence of the paranormal would never be questioned.

CITY HALL

In 1895, Davenport, Iowa, built an ornate new city hall while the rest of the country was in economic depression. The city outgrew its original facility, which had been located on Brady Street from 1857 to 1858.

The new city hall, to be located on the northeast corner of Harrison Street and West Fourth Street (226 West Fourth Street), was constructed without issuing any bonds. The cost was around $90,000, which was a monumental amount of money at that time.

How did Davenport do that when the rest of the country was financially hurting? By taxing booze and brothels. The fines levied against the city's houses of ill repute accounted for $7,000 to $9,000. The rest of the revenue came from a new state law, which applied to the city's 150 illegal saloons and taverns. The funds brought in from that law amounted to around $50,000 a year.

The taxes from both illicit activities allowed for construction of the new city hall and also paved the streets. From 1902 to 1908, the city eliminated property taxes altogether, according to the book *The Freedom of Streets: Work, Citizenship and Sexuality in a Gilded Age City*, by Sharon E. Wood.

The new city hall was designed by Davenport architect John W. Ross and built by Morrison Bros. Construction Company. The 60-by-145-feet, four-story building is constructed of Ohio Berea sandstone in the Richardsonian Romanesque style. A hipped roof caps the top, and the heavy stone helps support the weight of the steel frame. The structure includes corner towers, gable ends, rustic stone and Roman arches. Three stories of windows line

Built in 1895, Davenport's city hall, located at 226 West Fourth Street, is a four-story structure constructed of Berea sandstone in the Richardsonian Romanesque style. The ghost of a hanging man has been spotted in the clock tower. *Photo by Michael McCarty.*

the front of the building. There is also a cone-shaped roof, tower roofs and a large clock tower above the entrance.

Davenport City Hall is listed in paranormal books and websites because of several sightings of an apparition of a hanging man. This spectral figure can be seen when the moon is full.

"People say someone was hanged there," said Kyle Dickson. "I've done my research and it was just a rumor, a legend, because the jail was just built, two blocks away."

The Scott County Jail, located at 400 West Fourth Street, was built in 1897. Executions weren't held at the Davenport detention facility but carried out at the Iowa State Penitentiary in Fort Madison, Iowa. Plus, there are no records of any hangings at city hall.

There are a few stories floating around about an alleged hanging at city hall. "One of the stories says that the police were using it as a jail," Dickson said, "and apparently one guy was particularly bad, so they hanged him in the bell tower. Kind of a vigilante justice, no trial or anything—just hanged him."

According to another story, someone committed suicide in the bell tower. "There's no actual evidence of anyone hanging or being hanged in the tower," Dickson said. "It might have been just a legend."

Of the two stories, the suicide possibility makes more sense, since suicidal individuals have been known to jump or hang themselves from tall buildings. There is, however, one person who did die at the Davenport City Hall, though not from suicide.

"There was once a man named Hal and he was very upset with Davenport's city government," Dickson stated. "He tried to run for alderman during the 1970s and lost very badly to the incumbent. Hal went to every city council meeting and city board meeting. During one of those sessions, he had a heart attack and died right in the middle of it."

Dickson noted that many former mayors have said they've seen Hal on multiple occasions in their offices. "They see a ghost and they believe it to be Hal, who was known to be a heavy cigar smoker. It probably led to his demise. City officials swear they smell cigar smoke in the chamber, in the board meetings."

Davenport City Hall has been smoke-free for decades.

THE SOURCE BOOK STORE

If you stroll downtown Davenport and walk past 232 West Third Street, there would be no doubt in your mind that the quaint brick building was the storefront for the Source Book Store, often called the Source by customers. The giant display window clearly says in big red letters: Music, Books, Movies.

The Source, Iowa's largest and oldest used bookstore, was started by George Pekios in 1939. When he passed away, his son, Bob, managed the store. Now his grandson Dan, who represents the third generation of Pekioses, runs the business. "We have been in continuous business for eight decades now," Dan said with a proud smile.

The store's original location was where the Irish memorial statue is outside the Davenport Bus Depot and Scott Community College Urban Center. In the 1970s, the Source moved to Third Street.

"When I was little, my family lived outside of the Quad-Cities, but my mother and I would come to Davenport every weekend to see my Greek grandmother," said coauthor Mark McLaughlin. He added:

> Sometimes, while my mother and grandmother were cooking together, I would walk down to the Source to buy some books. George Pekios was a wonderful man. He was a grandfatherly, bearded fellow, and he would sometimes read to me from a book of poetry he wrote called Sonnets from the Peloponnese. It was a slender, self-published hardcover back

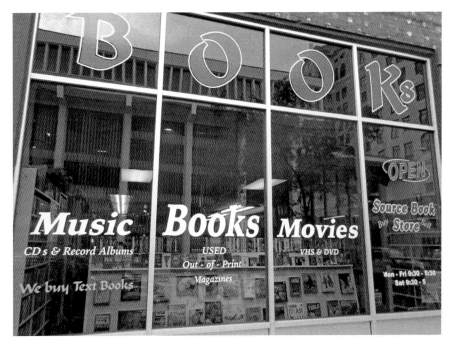

The storefront for the Source Book Store located at 232 West Third Street, downtown Davenport. It is Iowa's largest and oldest used book store. *Photo by Michael McCarty.*

The basement of the Source. *Photo by Michael McCarty.*

then, and I see that someone, no doubt the family, has since released it as a paperback on Amazon. Mr. Pekios was a very kind man, and he'd always chuckle at my love of scary books. He'd then suggest a few scary books for me to buy. I recall that I bought my very first book of H.P. Lovecraft stories at the Source.

Today, more than 100,000 items are in stock at the Source Book Store. "We buy, sell and trade used books, DVDs, CDs, vinyl records and vintage magazines," Pekios explained. The love of the written word is very evident in the bookshop, with over five thousand square feet of used, antique and out-of-print books packed with fiction and nonfiction publications from ceiling to floor on the first level and in the basement, too.

"I've been going to the Source Book Store for years," noted coauthor Michael McCarty. "I've known both Dan Pekios and Cheryl Minard Raley-Kirk for a long time. Some of the coolest books I've owned came from there. Doesn't matter if you just want to go window-shopping, or if you're a hardcore collector—this place has plenty to offer. I was surprised to discover that the place was haunted."

The subject of the haunting came up while Mike was talking with Dan Pekios about the sign warning about ghosts posted on the basement door. "Back in the late 1990s, I asked Dan why he had that posted," Mike said. "He told me it was because the basement was haunted."

The proprietor explained that he had noticed dark, eerie shadows in the corners. He had also heard unusual sounds. He also noticed that a chair would move to different parts of the basement whenever he would check the inventory down there.

"Everything he told me was intriguing," McCarty said.

So I asked permission to go down into the basement to investigate for myself. The stairwell was narrow and steep, and the basement was dark and crammed with books. I went from room to room in that part of the building, below ground level. I didn't really come across anything unusual or out of the ordinary, until I reached the very last niche that I hadn't visited yet. I found myself in front of an old furnace and it suddenly kicked in, giving me quite a scare.

McCarty chuckled to himself at the time, amused by the fact that an old furnace could give him a scare. "There I was, thinking that I had let my imagination get the best of me," he said. "But then I thought about it for a moment and I realized—it was summer time. Why in the world would the furnace suddenly kick in, in the middle of summer?"

McCarty made his way back upstairs and mentioned the incident to both Pekios and Raley-Kirk. They both said that furnace hadn't worked for years. "I went back downstairs," McCarty said, "and I touched the old furnace. It was stone cold."

Since that time, Pekios has ordered renovations to the basement. The general public no longer has access to the old furnace. The employees commonly refer to the spirit as "Grandpa"; others just call him "George." Whatever you call him, his presence is especially felt in the bookselling establishment's basement and dark corners.

"If I had to guess the identity of the ghost," McLaughlin said, "I would probably say it was George Pekios. He was a wonderful man who dearly loved all his books. He had a lively sense of humor, so it would be easy to imagine his ghost kick-starting that furnace to startle Mike, just for a laugh!"

THE ROCK 'N' ROLL MANSION

The Rock 'N' Roll Mansion is the nickname of the Townsquare Media Quad Cities headquarters at 1229 North Brady Street, Davenport, Iowa. The Mansion houses the radio stations 97X (WXLP 96.9 FM,) KIIK 104.9 FM, B100 FM, KBOB 1170 AM and ESPN QC 93.5 FM. Originally, this ominous, daunting brick building was once the Hill & Fredericks Mortuary, built in 1929 shortly before the stock crash of that year.

In the 1980s, the building became the home of a radio station. The fact that the Rock 'N' Roll Mansion was once a mortuary, with an imposing, eerie exterior, has been used for promotions—especially during the Halloween season. During one promotion, a local disc jockey was buried in a casket at dusk for an evening broadcast. His casket featured an air tube, of course. His below-ground broadcast lasted until sunrise.

One of the Rock 'N' Roll Mansion's most popular programs is *The Dwyer & Michaels Show*, starring Bill Dwyer and Greg Michaels. On their show, they've talked about the Crybaby Bridge, featured in this book in its own chapter. They've also parked a hearse in front of the station, with the words, "'mortician's transition" and "formaldehyde ride" marked on the vehicle.

"Those words on the hearse inspired R.L. Fox and myself when we wrote the song, 'Carnival of Souls' for the Quad Cities band, Beach Party Zombies," said Michael McCarty.

On October 31, 2015, members of the team Rock Island Paranormal spent the night at the Rock 'N' Roll Mansion to investigate the place for

Townsquare Media Quad Cities headquarters, located at 1229 North Brady Street, Davenport. The Rock 'N' Roll Mansion houses the radio stations 97X (WXLP 96.9 FM), KIIK 104.9 FM, B100 FM, KBOB 1170 AM and ESPN QC 93.5 FM and is guarded by two giant gargoyles created by Storehouse Peddlers. *Photo by Michael McCarty and Bruce Walters.*

any ghostly activity. Over the years, DJs and employees at the mansion have reported the elevator mysteriously moving between floors with no occupants. They've also heard the sound of footsteps when no one was around.

Rock Island Paranormal was formed in 2006 to help homes and businesses. According to the group's Facebook page, "We use various scientific methods to collect and analyze data to help us prove or disprove a 'haunting' or possible paranormal activity." Since the team's inception, members have worked with the Rock Island Arsenal, the Moline Parks Board, the Scott County Parks Board and other organizations.

Rock Island Paranormal brought members of the news station WQAD crew to the Rock 'N' Roll Mansion to video-record the overnight event. "We were interested in the place because it used to be a mortuary. That really got to us," said Ariel Renee Young of Rock Island Paranormal. "Founding member Jason Hess knew Dwyer and Michaels."

According to Young, Jason asked Dwyer if the Rock Island Paranormal team could visit. "Of course, we were able to get in, which was amazing," she said. "There were also a couple people who'd won contests who joined us on the investigation as well."

That evening's event brought surprising spectral developments.

"There was this little boy we talked to," Young said.

> *He wouldn't give us his name. With our K2 (an electronic magnetic energy detector), we followed him. He led us upstairs to a crawlspace by the rafters. Jason had already put cameras up there, because there were reports of someone running across the rafters. We found out it was the little boy that kept doing this. He admitted that it was where he likes to play.*
>
> *We caught a couple things on camera. In the basement in the file room, we saw the shadow of a man walking by. You could see his head and shoulders, but you couldn't see the bottom of him, which was really neat. We also caught a couple of orbs, too.*

Young has her own theories on why some places attract more paranormal activity than others. "I think sometimes it depends on location," she said. "Sometimes it depends on what has happened there. Places with a lot of limestone involved have a lot of activity. I'm not sure why—perhaps it's an energy thing. If there was a tragic event that took place, there's a lot of activity as well."

Rock Island Paranormal holds ghost tours of local cemeteries during the summer months. "We give plenty of history when we are there," Young said. "It's one of the big things that we do."

St. Ambrose University

St. Ambrose University started out as the St. Ambrose Academy, a Davenport, Iowa seminary and school for men, in 1882. John McMullen, the first bishop of the Catholic Diocese of Davenport, founded the school.

The school initially held classes in two classrooms in the school building at St. Margaret's Cathedral, the first Catholic cathedral in Davenport. It was eventually replaced by Sacred Heart Cathedral on the same block, which is now located at 422 East Tenth Street. The first class had thirty-three male students between the ages of twelve and twenty-three. Their tuition was only three dollars a month.

In time, the school moved to its current campus location on Locust Street in Davenport, and Ambrose Hall was the first building constructed on the new grounds.

Women started taking classes on the St. Ambrose campus in the 1930s, and in 1968, the institution officially became coeducational. In 1977, St. Ambrose first offered graduate classes, starting with the H.L. McLaughlin Master of Business Administration program. That same year, it was listed in the National Register of Historic Places.

In 1987, St. Ambrose College became St. Ambrose University and was organized into colleges of arts and sciences, business and human services. In 1997, St. Ambrose offered a doctor of business administration program.

St. Ambrose University, located at 518 Locust Street, Davenport, is famous for the statue of St. Ambrose in front of Ambrose Hall. Beginning with the first statue to stand guard on the front lawn of the campus, an unofficial tradition developed of painting the patron saint green around St. Patrick's Day to get everyone in the Irish spirit. These days, the statue is sheathed in green cloth every year on March 17. *Photo by Michael McCarty.*

In 2013, St. Ambrose University initiated a $5 million renovation project to restore St. Ambrose Hall and bring it back to an authentic late nineteenth- and early twentieth-century look. Among the many upgrades, the bell tower and spire were restored. A clock, depicted in the original plans but never installed, was added during the renovations.

St. Ambrose University is known for its robust school spirit—but is the school a home for any spirits from beyond?

"People have seen flashing lights in St. Ambrose Hall and have smelled the scent of incense burning," said Kyle Dickson. "There have also been reports of strange noises being heard randomly throughout the place."

According to the SAU Media Hive blog, the Iowa Paranormal Advanced Research Team performed an investigation of Ambrose Hall in 2007. While no conclusive evidence was uncovered, what they did learn was certainly compelling. The blog stated that "their evidence included EVP's [electronic voice phenomenon, the process of hearing a dead person's voice through electronic means] where a voice is heard saying, 'There is something wrong with me.' Also sounds of knocking, the smell of incense, cold chills, and orbs floating were all captured or documented."

Author Michael McCarty has researched the history of St. Ambrose extensively in search of paranormal possibilities. "I've heard rumors that a priest died there," he said. "I'm not sure if that is true or not, but that has been said several times over the years. I've also heard that a student committed suicide there but cannot substantiate whether or not such an incident has ever led to a haunting."

McCarty has personally experienced the unearthly on the St. Ambrose campus:

> *When I was a driver for Domino's Pizza, back in the 1980s, I needed to make a delivery at one of the dorms at St. Ambrose. I didn't know the campus that well, and thought that St. Ambrose Hall was the dorm I needed to visit. Boy, was I wrong about that!*
>
> *I walked up and down the hall that night, looking for where I thought I had to deliver the pizza. At one point, it felt like someone was following me. I'd stop and look behind me, but no one was there. Then I'd start walking again. The feeling of being followed continued. I'd stop and look around, but still, no one was there. It was disturbing.*

McCarty went on to host a radio show at St. Ambrose's radio station, KALA 88.5 FM, from 1993 to 1994 with producers David Baker and Randy Popp. The show was called *KALA Presents the Arts*, and the station was based in the Galvin Fine Arts Center on the St. Ambrose campus.

"I never experienced anything of a paranormal nature while working in the Galvin Fine Arts Center, just great radio shows and great conversations," McCarty said, "so if there is a supernatural presence on the St. Ambrose campus, it apparently keeps to Ambrose Hall and doesn't stray to the other buildings. Since Ambrose Hall was renovated in 2013, I can only wonder if the restoration of the building has appeased the restless spirits rumored to dwell within."

Author Mark McLaughlin is a graduate of St. Ambrose, but during his time there, he never experienced any supernatural occurrences. He noted:

> *I would have to agree with Mike. If there was anything paranormal happening on the campus, it must have stayed in Ambrose Hall. I lived*

in both East Hall and Davis Hall, and never experienced anything supernatural. But then, that fact is in sync with the general belief that ghosts tend to stay in one place.

"The fact that ghosts usually stay in one locale is the very basis of this work, Ghosts of the Quad Cities. *For some reason, spirits seem to be bound to a particular locale in the majority of haunting scenarios. Perhaps it was the location of their death, or a place that held special significance to them, as we have mentioned elsewhere in this book.*

McLaughlin observed that spirits are known to travel in one very notable instance:

If ghosts are limited in the distance they can travel, for whatever reason, that might explain the phenomenon of possession. Spirits would need to use a living human body as their vehicle to leave the site of their haunting. The question is, would they have enough power, enough concentration, to actually commandeer another person's body?

Also, when possession is discussed, a new question is raised. Is the paranormal presence in question a human spirit, or an inhuman presence? Thankfully, possession by an inhuman entity is found more often in novels and movies, as opposed to real-world settings. I mention that because mass-media entertainment tends to make people think that ghosts have to be malignant or even a demon. But really, why should that have to be? As we have learned while researching this book, it is clear that ghosts, more often than not, are harmless and sometimes even benevolent.

"This is a good reason to think of ghosts in a positive way," McLaughlin added. "If we start thinking of ghosts as good and well-being, suddenly the concept of death becomes less frightening. It means that death is not the end, and that the hereafter is a concept to be thought of without fear."

PALMER COLLEGE AND MASONIC TEMPLE

Kyle Dickson, assistant director of the German American Heritage Center, is also the organizer of the Darker Side of Davenport haunted tours, and he is well versed in the history of how Palmer College of Chiropractic is linked to spiritualism.

"I've always said during my tours, that the history of chiropractic care and spiritualism are really entwined through Daniel David Palmer, who was an avid spiritualist," he said. "He claimed he learned how to do chiropractic care through a séance from a ghost. Palmer was very into spiritualism and very into ghosts."

The *Los Angeles Times* did an article about how the $15 billion chiropractic industry "owes its existence to a ghost." About seventy-seven thousand chiropractors treat more than thirty-five million Americans every year.

"At Palmer College, especially the Palmer Hall, security guards would see unexplained things move. Stuff like that," Dickens said.

The *Quad-City Times* did an article about local ghost stories on October 10, 2018, and noted that there have been claims, based at Palmer College of Chiropractic, of ghosts flying "around the ceiling in a lecture hall causing hanging lamps to swing back and forth."

Palmer's memoir, *The Chiropractor*, was published in 1914, after his death. In his memoir, he noted:

> *The knowledge and philosophy given me by Dr. Jim Atkinson, an intelligent spiritual being, together with explanations of phenomena, principles resolved*

Above: Palmer College of Chiropractic is the founding college of chiropractics and is located at 1000 Brady Street, Davenport. A wood and glass display case with three human skeletons. *Photo by Bruce Walters.*

Right: "The Foundation of Chiropractic" courtyard at Palmer College of Chiropractic. A bust of Dr. Daniel David Palmer, "Discoverer & Founder." Sculpture by George Barton. *Photo by Bruce Walters.*

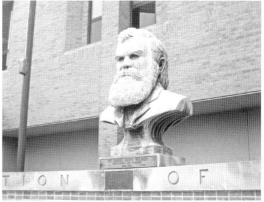

from causes, effects, powers, laws and utility, appealed to my reason. The method by which I obtained an explanation of certain physical phenomena, from intelligence in the spiritual world, is known in biblical language as inspiration. In a great measure The Chiropractor's Adjuster was written under such spiritual promptings.

The Chiropractor's Adjuster, also known as *Text-Book of the Science, Art and Philosophy of Chiropractic*, was another book that Palmer had written. Dr. Atkinson had been dead for more than half a century when he communicated with Palmer.

Palmer's intense spiritual connection could explain why Palmer College of Chiropractic, Phi Kappa Chi Frat House, the Old Masonic Temple and the nearby St. Luke's Hospital (now demolished, see the relevant chapter in this book) are said to have experienced so much paranormal activity over the years.

BUCKTOWN

onathan Turner, reporter for the *Moline Dispatch/Rock Island Argus/* QCOnline.com, wrote the book *A Brief History of Bucktown: Davenport's Infamous District Transformed*, published by The History Press in 2016. Bucktown is part of the eastern end of Davenport, Iowa, close to the Mississippi River. It's a good thing that Turner decided to chronicle that particular chapter of midwestern history, since few traces of that time remain today. Bucktown is now a conventional, growing section of Davenport, and no one would guess that it was once known as the "wickedest city in America."

Bucktown was settled by German immigrants, and at the turn of the twentieth century, it was a bustling, bawdy nightlife mecca, filled with bars, brothels, dance halls and theaters of high and low culture. When evening came, Bucktown crews and passengers of riverboats went there to party. Famed musicians Louis Armstrong and Bix Beiderbecke both performed in the Bucktown area.

As Turner recounted, Bucktown reigned notoriously over one hundred years ago as the city's infamous red-light district. That part of downtown, which borders Illinois, is again reclaiming a welcome high-profile role as an entertainment epicenter. Not only is it a place to eat, drink and be merry, but it is also an increasingly popular locus of commerce and residence.

Kyle Dickson noted that Bucktown is on the Darker Side of Davenport tour that he hosts. The tour presents attendees with an inside look at haunted locales in the city. Bucktown Center for the Arts, at Second Street and

Pershing Avenue, was the site of the famous Brick's Tavern. "James 'Brick' Munro was an entrepreneur and was very rich. He owned several different businesses, including a taxi service and a pavilion called Brick's Pavilion. He called it a goldmine," according to Dickson.

In the late 1800s, when Iowa tried to prohibit liquor sales, Scott County, Iowa (whose seat is Davenport), called itself "the free and independent state of Scott," Dickson noted, and ignored such laws. "Basically, nobody cared. The police all looked the other way."

"You couldn't drink in Iowa unless it was in the State of Scott. Scott County started a few provisions, like you could drink but not on Sundays. And with this, came the rise of Bucktown," he added.

The Rebirth of the Downtown Area

Roughly covering the area from Fifth Street to the river, and east of Brady Street to the Government Bridge on downtown's edge, the Bucktown neighborhood buzzed feverishly in the late 1800s and early 1900s. After years of neglect and abandonment, many historic buildings in the area today are finding new life, in a wide variety of uses—from new bars and other businesses to sleek, modern loft apartments that honor their home's architectural heritage.

"The Quad-Cities has not bragged about this enough—we were into the brewery thing way before it was cool to be in the brewery thing," said Kyle Carter, executive director of the Downtown Davenport Partnership, a division of the Quad Cities Chamber of Commerce. Carter added:

> *Blue Cat Brew Pub (Rock Island, Illinois) and Front Street opened in the mid '90s, before everybody else woke up. Not only was downtown in awful shape in both cases—Rock Island and Davenport—but those guys get major kudos for doing what they did, and they helped build a brewery fabric here that's hard to match. It's such a unique thing here, and the millennial generation loves it. Talk about retaining and attracting more talent—build more breweries.*
>
> *In the late 1800s, early 1900s, this place [Bucktown] was hopping. We really were the gateway to the West. I mean, St. Louis has nothing on this. It's a history that's largely been forgotten, and that's a real shame. I think it feeds into this complex in the Quad-Cities that we're not good enough.*

From the multimillion-dollar restorations of the 1915 Hotel Blackhawk and nearby 1931 Adler Theatre to transforming vacant warehouse buildings, many developers have helped bring the Bucktown area back to vibrant life.

"There is a leap of faith and risk involved in all of that. These developers have thought the risk was worth it, and so far, it's been paying off—preserving these historic buildings that are an integral part of the fabric of the community," Carter said.

Regarding generic commercial corridors with heavy traffic, he cited a hugely traveled Davenport thoroughfare:

> *Everybody's got a Fifty-Third Street. Every community in the United States of America has a Fifty-Third Street. They serve their purpose. They need to exist, but it doesn't provide character. There's no soul, no uniqueness. Downtowns, and especially our downtown, define us as a community. Visit another community when you travel, and the first place you go is downtown. And if it looks like a dump, you assume the rest of the community—whether it's true or not—is a dump, too.*

"You don't want that to be your impression to visitors or to residents. First impressions are valuable, from a community pride perspective," Carter noted.

> *They used to have bumper stickers in the '80s that said, "Last one out of the Quad-Cities, turn out the lights." That is no way to develop a community. Pride does matter. You can build a million Walmarts, but it's not going to set you apart. Everything in our downtown sets us apart—every little building, every little brick down there is unique to our little world, and that carries a lot of value.*

A history buff himself, Carter—in his downtown office across from the vacant 1920 Capitol Theatre—said of Bucktown: "It's so colorful, it's such cool stuff, and nobody knows it. Nobody knows how cool the history is."

"It was the birthplace of what became the Quad City Symphony Orchestra of today and the place where jazz was played on a regular basis," said film consultant Doug Miller of Davenport, who worked at the old RKO Orpheum movie theater (which became the Adler) in the 1960s.

"Brick Munro's Pavilion and Garden—Bucktown Center for the Arts today—was the hot spot where Al Jolson worked as a singing waiter before he became famous," Miller noted. "Jolson talked about his early days in

Bucktown before he made it big when he played the Burtis Opera House years later."

Near the spot where the first railroad bridge crossed the Mississippi River in 1856, the bustling railroads and river transportation put Davenport "at a big crossroads," he noted. "People wanted something to do, and people were looking for things that they maybe shouldn't do, since they were traveling and away from home," he said. "It went big about the same time-frame as Storyville, the red-light district in New Orleans."

"Walt Disney got turned down for a job three blocks from here, and the film history of this area, it's just fascinating stuff, and it's stuff we should be taking great pride in," Carter said. "We should use that past as a draw, a marketing tool to attract people to visit and live in the area. It gives Davenport identity, defines it. Talk about a badge of honor—who doesn't want to live in the wickedest city in America?"

Bucktown and Davenport's downtown area have come a long way over the years. And yet in the middle of all that growth, all that modern strategic development, there is still a place for the ghosts of the past. Ghosts don't limit themselves to Gothic manors and mausoleums. As you, dear reader, have seen from the other chapters in this book, the spirits of the past can be found throughout downtown Davenport. And certainly, there is no surprise in that. Ghosts can be found wherever people have lived, loved, laughed, fought and died.

THE SIN CITY OF THE MIDWEST

In the January 18, 1903 *Davenport Daily Republican*, Catholic bishop Henry Cosgrove used his pulpit to call upon all citizens to join a crusade "against gambling, prize fighting, all-night and Sunday saloons and their social evil."

"I have heard enough and I have been sufficiently told by men who travel and have the chance to know to convince me that we have a city here with worse conditions of immorality than any other in America," Cosgrove observed. "I believe from what I have heard that Davenport is the wickedest of them all. I don't like to sit still while it is going to the devil."

"Bucktown was known mostly for its brothels and booze," Dickson said. "Brick [Munro] didn't allow any prostitutes in his saloon. He would entertain over a thousand people some nights. Al Jolson, actor and the original jazz singer, worked there as a singing bartender during those days."

Dickson added that Bucktown was called the Tenderloin District for a funny reason. "The police who worked there were paid to look the other way, for which they did," he said. "Because of this, they were able to afford a fine cut of meat."

Dickson noted that while Brick made a lot of money, he ended up dying broke. "He helped everyone," he said. "He was very well-known for giving his money away."

So why does this once wicked corner of Davenport have a chapter in this book? In time, Brick's Tavern became known for being haunted. Apparently, the sins of the "wickedest city in America" still resonated in that locale long after the debauchery had ended.

"People would hear giggling and laughing as though a party was still going on, even when nobody was there," Dickson said. "You could hear *clink, clink, clink*—it was the madam of the night, counting the take in a cigar box."

Many thanks to Jonathan Turner for contributing additional research to this chapter.

CITY OF DAVENPORT CEMETERY

The Davenport City Cemetery is located off West River Drive, between Sturdevant and Division Streets. It's not known how many people are buried there, but there's a good reason why there are no exact figures. The cemetery was established in the early 1840s, and in 1881, the cemetery's office building burned down, along with the burial charts. Plus, the Davenport Public Library's city burial records go back to only 1882. Searching obituaries will not provide an answer, since obituaries weren't standard newspaper fixtures in this area in those days.

According to a representative of the Davenport Public Library's Special Collections Department, a total of six thousand burials would be a good guess. That figure takes into account 170 years' worth of burials on eleven and a half acres. These numbers also compare well with the number of people buried in other cemeteries that opened later.

Like all public cemeteries, the Davenport City Cemetery has had to deal with its share of care and maintenance problems. In a 2006 article, Alma Gaul of the *Quad-City Times* reported that the graveyard was being overrun by groundhogs, which needed to be trapped and removed. The newspaper has also reported on twenty-six grave markers that needed to be replaced, since the originals, dating back over a century, had deteriorated badly.

"The cemetery was a very interesting place," said Ariel Renee Young of Rock Island Paranormal. The group has kept the graveyard cleaned and restored and also carried out some investigations in the past. "You see things pop out behind gravestones. You hear disembodied voices. We've

Right: The City of Davenport Cemetery is eleven and a half acres, located between West River Drive, Sturdevant Street and Division Street in Davenport. *Photo by Michael McCarty*.

Below: The City of Davenport Cemetery was established in 1843. It is estimated that six thousand people are buried there, including veterans from the Civil War and the Spanish-American War. *Photo by Michael McCarty*.

seen unexplained shadows," she said. "We would like to do that place again, definitely."

Meanwhile, the Davenport City Cemetery is the site of a mystery that's far more intriguing than any groundhogs: the presence of burial mounds.

Some say they are Indian burial grounds, according to John Brassard Jr., coauthor with his father of the book *Scott County Cemeteries*. But old stories disagree on the reasons for the mounds. "Some say it was a cholera epidemic," Brassard said. "Some say it was a circus elephant that died in town and was buried there. Some say it was a group of Civil War soldiers. No one really knows for sure."

According to a 2004 article by Bill Wundram in the *Quad-City Times*, the mounds at the Davenport City Cemetery are reputed by legends to be cholera mounds from the 1870s, back when river towns were afflicted with the disease. The article notes that cholera was carried from port to port at that time. The bodies of immigrants who died from the disease on steamboats were often thrown overboard.

Even so, no excavations have been made in the mounds. The question of what they hold has never been answered. And so the mystery of what might be found within the mounds remains to this day.

St. Luke's Hospital

The History of St. Luke's Hospital

It might seem strange for any hospital to be a haunted locale, since hospitals are meant to be havens for healing. But as we all know, sometimes patients pass away at hospitals—it can't be helped. According to Wikipedia, "Some religious views argue that the 'spirits' of those who have died have not 'passed over' and are trapped inside the property where their memories and energy are strong." That property may well be the place where they died.

Also, sometimes hospitals may be built on the sites of previous hauntings. With time, a building can be repurposed, but who's going to tell the ghost that?

Daniel and Patience Newcomb originally built St. Luke's Hospital in 1866 as a private residence. Daniel was a farmer from New York who settled fifteen miles south of Rock Island, Illinois. His farm produced great amounts of corn, and in time, Daniel and his wife became quite wealthy. They built a house in Davenport—an Italianate-style home that included a spiral staircase made of walnut wood. Daniel and Patience never lived in the house, and it sat empty for years. It was said to have resembled Antoine LeClaire's house in East Davenport, built around the same time. Daniel and Patience also had a second home that was known as Brady Street Manor.

When Daniel Newcomb died, Patience donated the Italianate-style home to the Davenport Academy of Science. She was active in her efforts to help wounded soldiers and became the president of the Soldier's Aid Society of Davenport. She was also one of the founding members of the Soldier's Orphan Home, also known as the Annie Wittenmyer House (see the Oakdale Cemetery chapter for more details). In addition, she worked for the Presbyterian Church.

In 1871, "she also donated money in memory of her husband for the construction of Newcomb Memorial Chapel at 16th Street and Fillmore," according to a July 31, 2017 article by Alma Gaul of the *Quad-City Times*. The article noted that "the Newcomb mansion became a hospital when it was purchased in 1893 by the Episcopal church and renovated as joint project of the Episcopal diocese, a group called the Iowa Christian Home Board and several Davenport doctors, according to a document nominating the building for city of Davenport landmark status in 1999."

St. Luke's Hospital opened on April 30, 1885, as a twenty-bed hospital. It was the second hospital in Davenport, following Sisters of Mercy Hospital in 1869.

St. Luke's was originally intended as an emergency hospital, with its operating room on the second floor. Surgeries all depended on the weather—whether the skies were sunny or filled with clouds. Without ample sunlight, there wasn't enough light for the doctors to perform surgeries on that floor.

In 1895, the hospital was renamed the Davenport Training School for Nurses. Two years later, the name changed again, this time to St. Luke's Hospital Training School. In 1903, the administrators added space for an additional fifty patients. By 1909, the hospital was treating 356 patients.

St. Luke's Hospital shortly before it was demolished, across the street from Phi Kappa Chi. *Photo by Cassie Steffen, courtesy of the Broadway Paranormal Society.*

St. Luke's Hospital Training School was abandoned in 1919, when a new hospital was built and opened at Bridge and High Streets in Davenport. Since then, the St. Luke's building has been demolished and is now a parking ramp.

THE BROADWAY PARANORMAL SOCIETY

Cassie Steffen, with her partners Angie Bull and Tom Sappington, founded the Broadway Paranormal Society in 2018. Steffen and her organization did several investigations of St. Luke's before the building was leveled. She found the place as part of her day job as a demolition supervisor for Valley Construction. She has an eighteen-year career history in the field with a zero-accident record.

Reporter John Marx's article about Steffen in the December 22, 2018 *Rock Island Argus*, "Demo Queen: Rock Island Woman Loves Tearing Down Buildings," mentioned several Quad Cities locations that the demolition and excavator operator has demolished, including, "Jumer's Castle Lodge in Davenport, the Watchtower Plaza in Rock Island and the Moline Depot."

"We had so many EVP (Electronic Voice Phenomenon) from that building," Steffen said of the St. Luke's building in an interview with Michael McCarty. An EVP is a process that makes it possible to hear a dead person's voice by electronic means.

Steffens has also communicated with the dead via a spirit radio, which is a gutted 1940s tube radio with LED lights inside, with a Bluetooth speaker and Echo Vox phone app for ghost hunters to communicate with the dead. "It makes a whole bunch of sounds and it keeps spitting out sounds," she said. "The spirits are supposed to be able to take those sounds and make them into words. With this app, we have direct responses with it."

Steffen recalled:

> One time, we had a group of eight people in the basement with us. We saw a shadow figure standing on the back wall. We all moved around to try to debunk it. Was it caused by one of us? It was definitely a human shape and wasn't any of us. One of our investigators, he started talking to it and it started moving closer to us. It came through the room it was in, and into the next room towards us. It stopped about halfway through the room. We had to get into that room to get out. Everybody was really freaked out about

that. We had a guest investigator from another paranormal team with us and he ran up the steps, through the building, out the door, and across the parking lot before he stopped.

Communicating with the Spirits

Another paranormal occurrence happened when the Broadway Paranormal Society tried to communicate with the spirits. "We were there every night after work, from 4:00 p.m. until 10:00 p.m., for three weeks straight," Steffen said.

> *Because we knew it was coming down, we knew we had a deadline. We wanted to collect as much evidence as we could.*
>
> *One night, we had three of our team members with an invited friend of ours. He brought his wife and his two kids, and we were on the first floor and I yelled out, "Can you make a noise for us?" And a door slammed above us. We couldn't tell which floor it was, because it was a three-story building. So I asked it to do it again, and it did it again. I asked it to do it again. If it could do it again, we would come up and try to find it.*
>
> *We were trying to play a game with it. "We'll come try to find you, if you can make that sound again." And the door slammed again and there was no wind that day. The place was pretty well closed up as far as windows go, and the doors were always locked because we didn't want anybody else getting in the building and contaminating our investigations. We were the only ones in the building.*
>
> *We went up to the second floor and asked again, "Can you make that noise again?" A door slammed above us. "Do it one more time and we're going to come up!" And it did it again. So, we went up to the third floor and one of my investigators, Tommy (Sappington), said, "Wait until I get to the other end of the hallway, so I can figure out where the noise is coming from." We had people on one end of the building and the other, so I waited and then I said, "Make that noise again," and a door right below us, on the second floor where we just were, slammed on his end of the building and Tommy about jumped out of his skin.*

"We never did debunk it," Steffen said.

We went down to try to debunk it as wind or something like that and were actually trying to find the door that would have made that noise. The Habit for Humanity had come in and taken out most of the doors, so there weren't very many doors left to try to figure out.

We went into the front part, which as an old part of the building—the original house from before it was turned into a hospital. We went into the old part on the second floor, and it was the guy we invited named Bill and myself. Bill and I were by one of the bathrooms. I was looking at one of the bathroom doors and I said, "Maybe it's this door." I always left my recorder on, because that building was good for EVPs. We caught so many EVPs. While I was standing there, right after I said, "Maybe it was this one," you can hear a man say "Annabelle" and that was interesting. Right below us was the kitchen to the old house, and we had several EVPs from the kitchen of a female. She said her name was Anna.

Broadway Paranormal Society experienced several communications with the dead. "Anna was always ready to talk and ready to communicate," Steffen said. "She always played with K2s." A K2 meter is a tool for detecting spikes in electromagnetic energy.

We had a lot of EVPs with her voice on them. Bill and his wife lead the EVP session. I had my recorder in my hand. Angie and some of my other investigators were on the other side of the closet pantry. It didn't have a door and was enclosed underneath the steps that lead up to the second floor. It was really a tightly closed cubbyhole, and we're all standing there, asking questions. Suddenly I could hear a woman talking in my ear as plain as day, but I couldn't tell what she was saying. But, she was saying a whole sentence. It was the first time I ever heard anything with my own ears, as far as a voice.

I stopped them and said, "Did you hear that?" and they said, "No." I said, "There was a woman talking in my right ear." We went back and listened to the recorders, and I'd caught it on my recorder and Angie's recorder. It was a woman's voice talking. I couldn't really tell what she was saying, but it was a full sentence, maybe more.

In the paranormal investigations circle, that incident would be categorized as a Class C communication.

"When we were there, everything was disconnected," Steffen noted. "The electricity had been cut. The gas line had been cut. I did the sewer and water myself. I knew the whole building was dead. There was construction debris lying around."

At this point in her interview with McCarty, Steffen said, "I'm going to pull up a recording that we caught because it is amazing. There were three other people with me at the time. All the doors were locked. Everything was all closed up. We were standing in the hallway and I set my recorder on the fire extinguisher box and I heard this."

She then played the recording for Michael McCarty.

"It was definitely a child's voice that said, 'I can't find it.'" McCarty stated. "You really can't make out if it is a boy or girl, but it is definitely a child."

The area where the hospital used to be is across the street from Phi Kappa Chi, while down the block is the old Masonic Temple. Up the block is the Palmer College of Chiropractic. "You have the Masonic Temple," Steffen said. "The Freemasonry lodge locations are known for a high level of activity. This might shed light on the Skellington Manor Event Center in Rock Island, which is also reported haunted and was a former Masonic Temple."

"This is just my theory of St. Luke's," Steffen said.

> It was a very early hospital. They needed a sunny day to do a surgery. If it were cloudy that day, they wouldn't do surgeries. I think all this activity is because of the deaths that happened at that hospital. Back when they couldn't treat things like they can do now, with modern medicine. I feel if they are medicated and they aren't in the right state of mind, and don't know what is going on. I think it makes it harder for them to pass or move on where they should be, and they get stuck.

Steffen remembered the day the building was demolished. "The day that it came down, Angie, Tommy and I drove by and we cried," she said, "because we were so attached to that building. I turned non-believers into believers from the evidence I got from that building—People who were 'no way,' laughing at me, some of the laborers who were helping me when we were doing the disconnect. I let one listen to the evidence and he was afraid to go in." The thirty-thousand-square-foot building was leveled for a parking lot.

St. Luke's Hospital is just a parking lot now, but the Broadway Paranormal Society has since found a new place to investigate: the Dan Vinar Furniture Store, located at 500 Twentieth Street, Rock Island. The *Rock Island Argus* and *Moline Dispatch* did a front-page story about the retail furniture store and the Broadway Paranormal Society investigation of the building on October 28, 2018.

PHI KAPPA CHI FRAT HOUSE

A fraternity house seems like an unlikely place for a haunting. In frat house movies like *Animal House*, the only figures clad in flowing sheets on the screen are the drunken students at the toga party. But in real life, there is a frat house in the Quad Cities known for housing spirits of a non-liquid variety.

Phi Kappa Chi, the fraternity house in question, is part of Davenport's Palmer College of Chiropractic. Established in 1969, the house is located at 723 Main Street, and it is perhaps one of the most famous haunted houses in the bi-state area.

This two-story student-housing residence is high on a hill, and during the day, it looks like a perfectly normal frat house. But *normal* is not a word often used to describe this building and its paranormal history.

From the 1970s into the early 1980s, Jim Arpy, reporter for the *Quad-City Times*, wrote a series of articles about the haunting of the frat house. Manifestations of the haunting included unearthly footsteps, typewriters typing by themselves, toilets flushing when no one was there, doors opening and closing in the night with no one seen coming or going and an eerie blue light seen in both the basement and attic.

"I like to joke that every fraternity has its secrets, but the Phi Kappa Chi house also has some mysteries!" said Kyle Dickson, who conducts the Darker Side of Davenport tours. These tours introduce Quad-Citians to many of the city's haunted sites, and the frat house is included. "People bring up the Phi Kappa Chi fraternity all the time, when they talk about haunted places in the Quad Cities," he added.

The Phi Kappa Chi fraternity, located at 723 Main Street, Davenport. The two-story residence has been a fraternity house at Palmer College of Chiropractic since 1969. *Photo by Michael McCarty.*

Some claim it is haunted by the ghost of a homeless man, brought inside due to freezing temperatures in the 1930s, back when it was a private residence. "There was a guy in the house who died during the winter. Unexplained snow tracks inside the house have been reported," Dickson said.

John Brassard Jr. wrote about the house in an October 2017 entry for his blog *The Kitchen Table Historian* (www.johnbrassardjr.com.) The article was titled "Was the Phi Kappa Chi House One of the Most Haunted Houses in Davenport, Iowa?"

"This is a fraternity of professional men who want to become doctors in their chosen field of Chiropractic," Brassard noted. "They're building reputations of respect and trust with both the community they live in and the wider world. They are quite possibly the very last people that you would ever expect to say that they live in what may have been one of the most haunted houses in the Quad Cities."

In his column, Brassard noted that once, some balcony doors in the fraternity house opened by themselves. The students inside, who were

The Phi Kappa Chi fraternity, located at 723 Main Street, Davenport. Photo taken at night. An orb appears near the tiki torch and window by the door. *Photo by Michael McCarty.*

having a conversation, closed the doors and blocked them with a chiropractic adjustment table. The students went back to their discussion—but then the doors opened again, pushing the heavy medical table out of the way.

The fame of the house has traveled outside of the Quad Cities. In May 1972, occult writer Irene Hughes, a well-known Chicago medium, came to investigate the house, according to a *Quad-City Times* article titled "A Ghost Chaser Unravels the Mystery of Davenport's 'Haunted House'" by Jim Arpy, which can be found in the Davenport Downtown Library's Special Collections.

"Allegedly psychic Irene Hughes said the ghost of the doctor was angry because they were practicing chiropractics, which was something that he didn't agree with," Brassard said. "It was in line with the thoughts of the times. Not every doctor was into chiropractics or agreed with the practice."

One such doctor's name was William A. Stoecks. "He was a prominent Davenport physician in the early 1900s," Brassard said. "He was president of the Scott County Medical Association. He was big into politics."

According to "Still Doing His Rounds: The Haunting of 723 Main Street," an October 30, 2014 blog posted by the Richardson-Sloane Special Collections Center of the Davenport Public Library, researchers discovered that Dr. Stoecks was listed on the property records of the house and he lived there until his death in 1961.

Irene Hughes wasn't the only celebrity to take an interest in the house. The Amazing Kreskin, a world-famous mentalist, has also investigated the frat house. In 1991, Michael McCarty, one of the coauthors of this book, visited the Phi Kappa Chi house as part of a project with Kreskin (see this book's introduction for more details).

"I first met the Amazing Kreskin when I worked at the Funny Bone Comedy Club in Davenport, Iowa," McCarty said. "I was working as a promotion coordinator. I needed to help Kreskin to find a location for a séance he wanted to do for the media. I needed to find a Quad City haunted house for the event. So, I arranged for his séance to take place at the frat house, since I'd read so many articles by Jim Arpy about it."

Local television news crews, newspaper reporters and even some DJs all attended the séance. Kreskin asked the Phi Kappa Chi students to sit around a large table and then demonstrated the kind of activities that would occur during a séance.

"The hair on the back of my neck stood up during the presentation," McCarty said. "I felt a sudden chill come over me. Something definitely felt unnatural about the place. I was against a far corner of the building, but I kept feeling like someone was behind me during the show, I even turned to look, but behind me was just the wall."

The mystery of Phi Kappa Chi is far from solved. The identity of the ghost has never been established—and for that matter, no one has ever determined if one ghost or many haunt the house. Since the deceased individuals who have been named as possible haunters have all been men, it makes one wonder if the house is a fraternity not only for the living but for the dead as well.

BETTENDORF, IOWA

THE ABBEY HOTEL
AND CENTRAL AVENUE

There are several famous haunted hotels around the country. One prominent example is the Stanley Hotel, located at 33 East Wonderview Avenue, Estes Park, Colorado. This huge, Colonial Revival–style structure was the inspiration for Stephen King's *The Shining* and was also the filming location for the 1997 television mini-series of the same name.

At one point in the hotel's history, housekeeper Elizabeth Wilson experienced an electrical shock during a lightning storm. She wasn't killed, but the incident did happen in room 217, which was where the dead lady in the bathroom is found in King's novel.

Another famous haunted hotel is the Shanley Hotel, located at 56 Main Street, Napanonch, New York. The hotel has been the subject of paranormal investigations and has been featured on the TV shows *Ghost Lab* and *Ghost Hunters.* Allegedly, this former bordello is too terrifying for any guests under the age of sixteen. Everyone else has to sign a waiver to stay the night. Guests who do spend the night receive a continental breakfast.

The Abbey, located at 1401 Central Avenue, in Bettendorf, Iowa, is now an addiction treatment center, but it was once a fine hotel, as grand as other fine establishments covered in other chapters, including Quarters One, the former Villa and the Hotel Blackhawk.

It's interesting to note that the Abbey is located on Central Avenue—a street known for its washwoman ghost. According to local urban legends, the spirit of a plump, middle-aged washwoman has been spotted wandering the avenue. These sightings date as far back as the late 1800s. Some say she appears with a wringer washer, while others say she carries an old washboard. Little is known about her, except that she will occasionally wander into a home and start doing the laundry.

According to an article by Richard Pokora of the *Quad-City Times*, the sisters of Our Lady of Mount Carmel, also known as the Carmelite Sisters, constructed their monastery in Bettendorf between 1914 and 1917.

The sisters came to the Quad-City area from Baltimore, Maryland. Funds to build their monastery came from private contributions from citizens of the Quad Cities. Their monastery was named the Regina Coeli Monastery. Translated from the Latin, Regina Coeli means "Queen of Heaven." Arthur H. Ebeling, a Davenport architect, designed the structure. Initially, the monastery featured 116 rooms, where the sisters lived in cells of eight by nine feet.

The Abbey Hotel, located at 1401 Central Avenue, Bettendorf, Iowa. On the rooftop, there is a statue of the angel Gabriel with his trumpet. The hotel is located down the street from sightings of the washwoman ghost, who has been reported since the late 1800s. *Photo by Michael McCarty.*

The Abbey Hotel originally was a monastery for Our Lady of Mount Carmel, also known as the Carmelite Sisters, constructed between 1914 and 1917. Often, members of the order who died were buried in a crypt beneath the altar in the chapel. *Photo by Michael McCarty.*

According to the article "From Monastery to Treatment Center" by Joseph L. Lemon Jr., "the sisters lived exclusively behind the monastery's imposing walls (13 sisters were buried in its crypt). Their primary occupation was to pray for the local community."

In 1992, the monastery became the Abbey Hotel. In 2007, the hotel became the Abbey Addiction Treatment Center.

The Villa de Chantal chapter addresses the public's fascination with individuals who follow a religious path, such as the sisters who once lived at the villa. That fascination can lead to the formation of urban legends. With those thoughts and facts in mind, it comes as no surprise that there have been reports of the Abbey being haunted.

Manifestations of that haunting have included cold spots, orbs and reflections appearing in photographs—and strange voices in the middle of the night. The question is, are these manifestations real or the result of overactive imaginations? Perhaps the presence of those who believe in the supernatural *allows* those believers to perceive the otherworldly influence around them. In other words, maybe you have to believe in the paranormal before you can perceive it.

From a monastery to an elegant hotel to an addiction treatment center, the changes that have taken place at the Abbey have embraced a wide range of community objectives. Certainly, this grand structure has always been put to good use.

Moline, Illinois

RIVERSIDE CEMETERY

Riverside Cemetery in Moline, Illinois, is known for its picturesque terracing and sweeping view of the Mississippi River. Located at 800 Twenty-Ninth Street, it was founded in 1851 as the Moline Cemetery by Samuel and Mary Bell. It was also known as the Fourth Street Cemetery. The first sexton was Joseph Pershing.

When John Deere was mayor of Moline, the cemetery underwent numerous changes. In 1873, the city took over control, and the mayor and the city council appointed a board of directors. The name was changed to Riverside Cemetery, and over the years, it has expanded from its original size, five acres, to more than ninety acres.

The Riverside Mausoleum, a Greek Revival–style structure with stained-glass windows, was completed in 1916. The Moline City Council dissolved the cemetery's board of directors in 1978 and placed Riverside Cemetery under the guidance of the Park and Recreation Board.

Over the years, the land owned by the cemetery was sold off. Today, Riverside Cemetery consists of sixty-two acres. This area does not include the land between the upper and lower cemeteries. This land is now used as Riverside Park.

Riverside is the final resting place of approximately twenty-eight thousand people, including Mayor John Deere, also world-famous as an inventor and industrialist; Willard Velie, an industrialist who developed advanced engines for automobiles and airplanes; musician Louie Bellson; Warren Giles, Hall of Fame baseball executive; and Francis Dickens, son of author Charles Dickens.

Each September, a historical cemetery walk called Echoes from Riverside Cemetery is held. Costumed performers portray famed individuals buried in the cemetery, telling stories of their lives. A book based on the walk was published in 2010.

Francis Jeffrey Dickens was the third son and fifth child of Charles Dickens and his wife, Catherine Dickens. Francis was nicknamed "Chickenstalker" by his father after the character Mrs. Chickenstalker in the Christmas book *The Chimes*. Dickens was writing the book at the time of Francis's birth. Most people simply called him Frank.

Francis was born in England and went to school in Germany to become a doctor. But his career went in a different direction. He ended up working with the Bengal Mounted Police in India for seven years and Canada's North-West Mounted Police for twelve years as an inspector.

While Francis was staying at a hotel in Ottawa, Canada, he struck up a friendship with Moline residents Dr. Alexander Jamieson and his wife. Dickens was planning to embark on a series of lectures across America, an initiative his father had completed years before.

"He was going on a lecture tour to talk about his experience with the Canadian Mounties," said John Brassard Jr. In 1885, Francis Dickens was in charge of the defense of Fort Pitt on the North Saskatchewan River. The Cree tribe and Chief Big Bear outnumbered and outgunned the North-West Mounted Police. The chief gave Dickens and his men a short time to abandon the fort.

Dickens came to Moline to visit Dr. Jamieson and his family and start the lecture tour. He read to the Jamieson child from his father's works, and those books are still in the possession of Jamieson descendants.

According to Brassard, on the night of the first speech in Moline, "He had a sudden heart attack and died before he could give even the speech. He had no money, so the citizens of Moline took up a collection to help bury him." Dr. Jamieson's family also helped to finance Dickens's burial.

Dickens's relatives were eventually contacted about his burial arrangements. "His brothers and sisters said something like 'we'll go ahead and let him be buried where he lay.' My guess is they didn't want to pay the money to ship his body back," Brassard said.

"In 2002, the Canadian Mounties added a second gravestone with the North-West Mounted Police logo on it and gave him a service with bagpipes and all. So that is why he has two tombstones at Riverside," he added.

Ariel Young of the investigative team Rock Island Paranormal noted that the group has performed investigations in the cemetery. "The pauper section gets the most activity," she said. "If you go there, make sure to bring devices to hear things." The things she mentioned include EVP, sounds considered to be spirit voices recorded either by accident or intentionally.

Riverside Cemetery is associated with two ghost stories. One involves a moving grave marker and the other a statue known as the Black Angel.

There have been reports of a tombstone on the top of a hill that will glow during the night. There are also rumors that the tombstone will turn 180 degrees and face the opposite direction.

"I've heard the story of the revolving tombstone," said Brassard.

> But, I haven't found anything concrete—no pun intended—about it. Right now, I have to conclude that it's just a cool story that someone made up, like the Black Angel's death curse.
>
> There are a lot of stories around the country of haunted tombstones that glow, jump, curse and more. I'm pretty sure there's probably one out there that will start your car and wash your windows, if you look hard enough. However, that's not to say that there aren't some compelling tales out there with some basis in fact.
>
> For example, there is a revolving tombstone in Mt. Carmel Cemetery in Chicago. It's big and made of stone, but it's actually designed to turn 180 degrees. Who knows—there might have been something like that out at Riverside at one time.

The Black Angel was a memorial for Charles H. Deere, a president of John Deere Company and son of John Deere. "It was a big memorial," said Brassard. "It had a giant cross with a female angel statue standing in front of it, with a series of steps by it. It is like the other Black Angels in the area."

There are Black Angel statues at the Ruth Anne Dodge Memorial at the Fairview Cemetery in Council Bluffs, Iowa, and also the Feldwert Memorial at Oakland Cemetery in Iowa City. To learn more about the Black Angel in Iowa City, read *Haunted Iowa City* by Vernon Trollinger.

The Black Angel of Riverside has inspired many urban legends. "The story was, if you kissed it at midnight, you died. There are other stories, too," Brassard said.

There is even an urban legend about a young lady who stayed all night by the Black Angel. In the morning, it was revealed that her hair had turned completely white.

Rick Lopez, the co-owner and chef of Igor's Bistro, featured in a different chapter, has heard about the Black Angel and Riverside Cemetery, and he noted that the story he heard goes like this:

Some boys and girls were at a graduation party one night, a long time ago. Riverside Cemetery was just down the street and they were talking about how scary it was. "Don't ever stand on a grave after dark," one of the boys said. "The person inside will grab you and pull you under."

"That's not true," one of the girls said. "It's just superstition."

"I'll give you a dollar if you stand on the Black Angel's grave," said the boy.

"A grave doesn't scare me," said the girl. "I'll do it." So the children started for the Riverside Cemetery.

The graveyard was filled with shadows and as quiet as death. "There's nothing to be afraid of," the girl told herself, but she was scared nonetheless. The kids soon came upon the Black Angel, with wings spread out and arms welcoming. The boys being boys, they soon scattered and returned to the party, leaving the girl all alone in the cemetery.

The girl, not wanting to be labeled a "scaredy-cat," went to stand on the grave. Just then, there was a flash of lightning and a crack of thunder, which proved too much for her. She started to run but couldn't move, for she was filled with terror.

"Something has got me!" she screamed, falling to the ground. She was found the next day, sprawled across the grave. Her sweater had been caught on a tree branch that held her back.

According to Brassard, the area around the Black Angel was basically a nice quiet spot where you could take your girlfriend for an amusing scare. "Kind of like a precursor to today's horror movies. Most of the stories were nonsense. In my family, my grandfather took my grandma up there and made her kiss the Black Angel. She lived and they were married for another forty years," he said with a laugh.

In June 1965, according to local newspapers, vandals doused the Black Angel with orange and green phosphorescent paint. Later, in the early 1970s, "The Deere family got tired of the vandalism," Brassard said. "It was moved to the Deere Wiman House [also known as the Butterworth Center at 1105 Eighth Street, Moline]. Some people said it was in the garden. Some people say it was in the basement. The family moved to Santa Barbara, California, and they had the Black Angel shipped out there."

According to a 2003 article by John Willard of the *Quad-City Times*, Patricia Hewitt, a descendant of John Deere, had the statue moved to Santa Barbara. The metal statue now can be found at the Mandala Center, a retreat at the slopes of the Sierra Grande Mountain near Raton, New Mexico.

Rock Island, Illinois

JOHN LOONEY MANSION

John Looney—lawyer, newspaper publisher and gangster—is the most infamous crime figure to come out of the Quad Cities. He has been called "The Al Capone of the Quad Cities," but technically, Looney was an organized crime leader out of Illinois before Capone.

Looney started his career as a lawyer, but eventually he gave in to the allure of crime. He also used his newspaper, *Rock Island News*, to further his criminal goals. His checkered life was the inspiration for Muscatine, Iowa author Max Collins's 1998 graphic novel *The Road to Perdition*. In 2002, the graphic novel was turned into a movie of the same name starring Paul Newman, Tom Hanks and Jude Law. The motion picture grossed more than $180 million. Also, the nonfiction book *Citadel of Sin: The John Looney Story*, by Richard Hamer and Roger Ruthhart, details the rise and fall of Looney.

The Rock Island gangster was the subject of a *Dead Files* episode. In this television series, Steve DiShiavi, a retired New York police detective, and paranormal researcher and medium Amy Allen investigate true hauntings and other things that go bump in the night. Looney owned several properties in his lifetime. The house investigated by *Dead Files* was on the bluffs overlooking the Rock Island Fitness and Activity Center, far from Looney's Bel Air home, although the land might have been part of that property. That area was undeveloped back then.

The Looney mansion is one of the most interesting historical and architectural residences in Rock Island, Illinois. This Queen Anne–style house, located at 1635 Thirtieth Street, was built in 1895, has three floors and over five thousand square feet. It was once owned by gangster John Looney. *Photo by Michael McCarty.*

No reported haunting occurred at the main Looney mansion, located at 1635 Twentieth Street, Rock Island. The house was originally Looney's residence, then turned into apartments, then converted back to a single-family dwelling.

"*The Dead Files* did a piece on Looney, and I question the accuracy of the reporting," author Roger Ruthhart said.

> *They had a house that was built on land Looney at one time owned. Owners claimed the house was haunted, and it may have been, but I doubt if it was haunted by Looney. The house was miles from where Looney actually lived and the "haunted" house wasn't even built until decades after Looney had died. There is no real reason to think he would haunt it, as opposed to other homes he owned. There were three here and others elsewhere. I was interviewed for more than an hour by the show, spelled out all the historical details, and they selectively edited it to make it sound like I was supporting their theory, which I wasn't.*

As I said, Looney had three homes here, as well as his ranch in New Mexico and other homes he lived in during his life. I have heard no stories about any of them being haunted. If there were, it certainly would have been in the book.

According to Ruthhart, Looney "controlled a vast and unmatched empire of extortion, bribery, booze, gambling and prostitution." For the first quarter of the twentieth century, "his power in Rock Island grew almost absolute, because he was able to control portions of two key elements of society—politicians and the press. Member of his organization controlled elements of his crime business. Looney published the *Rock Island News* from 1905 to 1923. There were downtown shootings, political graft and bombings, as well as his scandal-sheet newspaper." In 1922, six murders in Rock Island were all tied to Looney.

Looney used lies and slander in his newspaper to blackmail community leaders and brutality and violence to enforce his will. In 1912, things came to a head with Looney and Rock Island mayor Harry Schriver. "Looney attacked the mayor in a series of articles in the *News*," Ruthhart commented in his book. Eighteen newsboys were arrested, and their newspapers were confiscated.

According to Ruthhart, Schriver had Looney brought to the police station, where he beat him as police officers watched. Looney was hospitalized.

"The next night, March 27, 1912, Looney's gang convened a meeting in Market Square," Ruthhart noted. "The crowd grew to more than 2,000 and the angry mob stormed the police station and the police fired back, killing two bystanders and wounding eight others. Martial law was declared and the governor sent in 600 troops to quell the riot." The military remained in Rock Island for nearly a month until after the election. Looney left town and moved to New Mexico for nine years.

"He returned in March 1921, revived the *News* and re-established his control over local vice. Looney controlled almost all the gambling and prostitution houses, about 150 over a vast region, run by Helen Van Dale, known as 'Queen of the Prostitutes.' This time around, he added corrupt police, judges and city officials to the list of things he controlled," Ruthhart stated in his book.

The book also noted:

While John Looney rose to power by blackmail and gunfire, it was also his downfall. When Looney raised the "protection fee" charged to Bill Gabel, a former police officer who owned one of the city's largest bootleg saloons, Gabel refused to pay. Instead he turned over 12 cancelled checks made out to Looney to federal investigators.

Gabel met with agents at the Como Hotel on July 31,1922. He was getting out of his car just after midnight when shots were fired. One bullet hit him in the head and he died instantly. Drive-by shootings had become commonplace. On Oct 6, 1922, John Looney's one-time lieutenant, Dan Drost joined forces with Anthony Billburg, another lieutenant turned enemy. With two other men, they ambushed Looney and his son Connor and bodyguard outside the Sherman Hotel. John Looney fled to the hotel, while his son Connor, 21, returned fire before he slumped to the ground. He died the next day. The four men were sent to prison for the murder.

By October 26, 1922, all of Looney's saloons and brothels were closed. Six stills were destroyed. His houses were raided and his arms cache seized. The News *ceased publication. A federal investigation revealed that 170 or more illegal businesses had been paying for protection from Looney.*

After his son's funeral, John Looney fled to New Mexico. Federal conspiracy charges were filed against him. Federal prohibition authorities joined state, county and city law-enforcement officers in an anti-vice campaign to clean up the community. John Looney was captured in Belen, New Mexico, on November 30, 1923 and returned to Rock Island, Illinois. He was sentenced to prison for conspiracy and the murder of Bill Gabel. Looney was released from prison in ill health in April 7, 1934, at age 68 and never heard from again. He died March 4, 1942.

There were too many fascinating things about Looney's life to fully cover in one chapter, including the bombing of his newspaper in 1908. To learn more, please read *Citadel of Sin: The John Looney Story.*

"While John Looney had several homes and properties, his mansion overlooking the Rock River called Bel Air was famous for the weekend parties, drunken orgies and nude swimming in the Rock River, as well as cock fights, boxing and bulldog fights," Ruthhart said.

The Dead Files did its show about a property that Looney once owned near the Rock River. No reported haunting ever occurred at the Looney mansion, located at 1635 Twentieth Street, Rock Island. The building was converted to Hillcrest Apartments in 1939 and was an apartment building for over fifty years. It was eventually turned into a single-family home. "That place been remodeled so many times, any ghosts that might have been lurking there are probably gone," Ruthhart said.

The Looney house is located at the entrance to the Highland Park Historic District. According to the publication *Highland Park Historic District: History & Architecture*, Looney liked the Queen Anne house that belonged to his next-door neighbor and former law partner, Frank H. Kelly. In fact, Looney liked the house so much he arranged to have a similar home built for himself by Rock Island architect George P. Strauduhar (who also designed the Villa de Chantal, just up the street from both houses).

The Looney place is three stories tall and with appropriately five thousand square feet. *Highland Park Historic District* described the place as having a gray stone veneer, very rare in Rock Island residences. Another distinctive feature of the Looney mansion is the porches. The first-floor porch wraps around the south and west walls, with classical Tuscan columns. There are also porches on the second floor. The French clay–tiled roof, rugged chimneys and arched opening under the porch give the structure a brooding appearance.

"I lived next to the John Looney mansion for two decades," said coauthor Michael McCarty.

> I was inside the house on three occasions. The first was when it was up for sale, back in the late 1990s. The second time, during the summer of 2010, I took a tour with my friend and fellow writer Joyce Godwin Grubbs. And the final time, before the house was sold again, the homeowner allowed me to have another look at the house.
>
> It was during the summer, and the homeowners, Ray and Vonnie Berger, were getting ready to move. Mrs. Berger was the only member of the family who was home at the time, and she gave me permission to look around as she was watering her garden. I went into the basement to do research. I wanted to see if the stories were true—that there were secret tunnels that ran between Looney's house and the home of Frank Kelly.
>
> While I was in the basement, I was inspecting the space under the steps, when I heard someone walking down the steps directly above me. I quickly came out to see who had entered the basement, but no one was there. I walked back outside and Mrs. Berger was still watering her flowers. I asked if she'd been inside, and she said she'd been outside gardening the whole time.

Side note to this story, although McCarty didn't find hard evidence that there were tunnels inside the Looney residence, there were several local newspaper articles and even a special news story on Channel 4, WHBF, about the District catacombs, which had direct links to Looney's legal and illegal businesses in downtown Rock Island.

McCarty noted that another unusual occurrence happened shortly after the homeowners moved out. The house was sold, but the new owner hadn't moved in yet. It was during the late summer, and there was a power outage in the Highland Park area of Rock Island. For hours, there was no power for several blocks.

McCarty recalled:

> *We were without electricity for more than eight hours. It was a typical "dog day" of summer, with temperatures in the 90s, leading into the 80s that evening. My wife and I, along with our pet rabbit, were extremely hot in the apartment. It was around midnight and I decided to go to the convenience store across the street to pick up some bottled waters.*
>
> *It was still cooler outside than inside the apartment. I remember, there was a huge moon up in the night sky. I was walking around the block and I stopped in front of the Looney house. On the third floor, there is a balcony and with the bright moon, I could see a shadow at the window. The place was empty, but I could see someone at the window, looking down at me. I walked a few more steps, then looked back. That shadow was still there. I walked a few more steps and turned around again—and the shadow was gone.*

While John Looney never garnered the fame and notoriety of Al Capone, the movie *Road to Perdition* and the book *Citadel of Sin* will help to make sure that Looney's fascinating legacy of crime will never be forgotten.

VILLA DE CHANTAL

The Villa de Chantal in Rock Island, Illinois, was once a solemn Catholic boarding school, a place of opulence and European sophistication. But in time, this impressive structure went up in flames, leaving behind intriguing urban legends about the souls that may have dwelled within.

According to a July 14, 2005 article in the *Rock Island Argus* and also the publication *Highland Park Historic District: History & Architecture*, the Sisters of the Visitation came to Rock Island from Maysville, Kentucky, in August 1899. They opened a private school on Fifth Avenue near Sacred Heart Church. But the cramped, confining quarters resulted in some of the students and the sisters contracting tuberculosis. Something needed to be done.

Two years later, the sisterhood decided to build a larger school and convent on what was known as Ball's Bluff, at the edge of Highland Park. From 1901 to 1958, the Sisters of Visitation operated the new facility, known as the Villa de Chantal. The Villa was a twelve-grade Catholic boarding school for girls ages five to eighteen, in classrooms that doubled as offices and dormitories.

The neo-Gothic design of the Villa was reminiscent of a European cathedral. Its ornate, baroque design featured slate rooftops, a variety of window sizes and shapes, octagonal towers and a belfry with a convent bell that the sisters had brought from Kentucky. The Villa was designed by Rock Island architect George P. Straduhar, who also designed the Looney and Kelly houses (discussed in the Looney chapter) about one block away.

The Villa de Chantal, located at 2101 Sixteenth Avenue, Rock Island, was designed in the Neo-Gothic style, reminiscent of a European cathedral. The school burned down during the summer of 2005. *Photo by Jill Doak, courtesy of the City of Rock Island.*

"The inside was just elegant," said Stephanie Smith of Milan, Illinois, who worked as a chef at the Villa back in the 1980s. "Stained glass windows, arches, oriental rugs, pillars, a grand piano—the works."

In 1919, the Villa forged an association with the North Central Association of High Schools and Colleges, resulting in increased attendance. By 1925, there was a major space shortage for students. Through impressive fundraising and generous donations, the sisters were able to add Lewis Hall, which was dedicated in 1930.

Then came the Great Depression and World War II, bringing hard times to the Villa. Alterations to the campus were minimal in the next two decades. In 1958, the decision was made to close the boarding school and focus on the Villa on operating as just a school. The last class graduated in 1975. In 1978, the Villa ceased operations.

In the early 1990s, the complex was sold and became a private school known as Morningstar Academy. The building was also available for parties and receptions. The school moved from the building in 2005. It was decided that the structure was going to be renovated into apartments for seniors. But, on July 14, 2005, a fire consumed the older sections of Villa de Chantal, burning most of the school down to the ground.

"I recall that it was a Thursday," said author Michael McCarty, who lived near Villa de Chantal at the time. This is what he observed:

> My neighbor called me while she was driving to work, to tell me that the neighborhood was smothered in black smoke. I went outside, and sure enough, that smoke she mentioned was everywhere. I heard the sirens and followed their direction. The Villa was ablaze, with fire trucks and police cars scattered around it. The news reported on the inferno all day.
>
> The next morning, I took a walk around the neighborhood. All that was left of Villa de Chantal was the brick shell structure. It was sad to see such a magnificent structure reduced to charred, ruined bricks and ashes.

The Rock Island–Milan School District acquired the property, and the remaining buildings of Villa de Chantal were torn down in 2008. In their place, the Rock Island Center for Math & Science opened in 2010.

Over the years, many ghost stories had popped up about Villa de Chantal. Many urban legends have been spun regarding supernatural goings-on at the Villa. It is said that nuns there became pregnant and would kill their unborn babies. They would then hide the bodies in the walls of the school. Students reported hearing babies crying, which tied in with the legends of the nuns. They would also hear disembodied screams and strange voices late at night. They also claimed to have seen objects moving by themselves. The place supposedly had a high number of student suicides over the years. It was said that they would jump to their deaths from a fourth-floor window.

John Brassard Jr. noted:

> I saw the blogs about that and people are still arguing about that. I think the whole story is nonsense. It might have been haunted. I don't know. I can't say that people didn't hear banging in the walls or heard voices in the middle of the night. The Villa burned down in 2005, so we may never know the truth. As far as I know, the cause of the fire was never determined.

"There was this nun," said Smith. "Before she became a nun, she'd been married for a very long time. She had fourteen children and when her husband died, that was when she became a nun. I am thinking how all these rumors started about the babies and the nuns. But they are untrue."

Still, it is not surprising that Villa de Chantal would be the focal point of urban legends. According to Wikipedia, an urban legend "is a form of modern folklore. It usually consists of fictional stories, often presented as true, with macabre or humorous elements, rooted in local popular culture. These legends can be used for entertainment purposes, as well as semi-serious explanations for random events such as disappearances and strange objects." In the case of the Villa, it is easy to see how such an imposing structure could captivate the imaginations of local citizens—especially since the building, founded by a sisterhood, held such religious significance in the area.

"As for the suicides," Smith said, "I never heard of any. Shortly before I worked there, there were two students who accidentally fell from the top of the fourth-floor staircase. It wasn't ruled suicide—they were accidental deaths."

People are often fascinated by religious orders, and rightly so: those who belong to such orders have dedicated their lives to the spiritual realm. It is understandable that imaginative folks might speculate on the lives of such pious individuals and make up stories to add more drama to the mix. The media bear witness to that drama. An article appeared in the *Sun* (www.mirror.co.uk) about the recent horror movie *The Nun*, titled "*The Nun* Set Was Blessed to Keep Demons Away—But Director Tells of 'Romanian Soldiers' Ghosts." The title pretty much says it all. Even when people create a fictional movie about a religious group, members of the public still feel it is necessary to extend the supernatural aspects of the fictional story into the real world.

There is just no suppressing the human imagination.

Many thanks to Jeff Ernst for contributing additional research to this chapter.

AUGUSTANA COLLEGE

ounded in 1860, Augustana College in Rock Island, Illinois, is a private liberal arts college of about 2,600 students. The hilly, 115-acre campus is located along the Mississippi River. The school has a 12-to-1 student/faculty ratio and is the home of WVIK, the flagship National Public Radio station for the Quad Cities.

Augustana College is also known as the home of some very special spirits.

Kai Swanson, special assistant to the president at Augustana, says that the ghosts of Augustana can be best described as "poignant." According to Swanson, one of these spirits said to be found on the Augustana campus is Apollonia Weyerhaeuser, one of the many children of lumber baron Friedrich Weyerhaeuser. The Weyerhaeuser house, located on campus, is now more commonly known as the House on the Hill.

Wikipedia notes that Friedrich Weyerhaeuser (1834–1914) was a timber mogul, the founder of the Weyerhaeuser Company and the eighth-richest American of all time. His company owned large areas of forested land, as well as sawmills, paper factories and other business enterprises. He married Sarah Elizabeth Bloedel in 1857, and they had seven children: John, Elise, Margaret, Apollonia, Charles, Rudolph and Frederick. Weyerhaeuser was buried in the family mausoleum in Rock Island's Chippiannock Cemetery.

According to a 1914 article in the *New York Times*, Weyerhaeuser died at age seventy-nine of a severe cold that developed threatening symptoms. The article stated, "The Lumber King had no diversions or recreations. His amusement, he used to tell his friends, was working."

This twenty-five-room Victorian mansion was once owned by lumber baron Frederick Weyerhaeuser. It is located on the Augustana College campus at 3052 Tenth Avenue, Rock Island. *Photo by Michael McCarty.*

His daughter Apollonia was married to Sam Davis, who ran the Iowa/Illinois Gas & Electric Company. Apollonia and Sam were the last members of the Weyerhaeuser family to live in the house. Their son Edward gave the house to the college in 1954, along with twenty-six acres of land. The house, a Second Empire–style mansion, can be found in the National Register of Historic Places.

"Faculty and students have lived in it," Swanson said. He noted that many stories have been told about the ghosts said to dwell within. "In some of the stories," he said, "the bathtub will be found filled to just under the overflow drain. Spigots will turn on and off. Doors will be jammed shut, and then unjam before the custodian can fix them."

It is said that Apollonia's brothers hated the well in the building's basement because it needed to be pumped manually. It is for that reason that the ghost of Apollonia will play with spigots—no doubt in memory of her brothers and their private war with the house's plumbing.

"Apollonia was a kind soul who loved the house," Swanson said.

Swanson shared another tale that told of Apollonia's gentle nature. One warm autumn day, a girl who'd been rejected by her boyfriend was sobbing. The young woman reported feeling a refreshing breeze. "She then decided she was going to be okay," he said. "After all, there were other fish in the sea! But where had that breeze come from? The windows weren't open."

At one point, some paranormal investigators spent the night in the House on the Hill, and Swanson was with them. "They have a device that reads energy levels," he said. "This device could also detect words being presented by the spirits, and words that appeared included 'umbrella,' 'red' and 'petra.'"

"'Petra' is Latin for stone, and it's also an ancient city in Jordan," Swanson said. "It's also the name of a girl I once dated." In fact, Swanson once sneaked into the building where Petra lived to visit her for a late-night study session.

Had the spirit of Apollonia read his mind?

Another supernatural presence said to be found on the Augustana campus is the ghost of Chauncey Morton, who was killed in a dorm on October 24, 1958.

"Chauncey was one of the few black students on the campus at that time," Swanson said. "A white student shot him while playing with a starter pistol. That student then dropped out of school."

Over the years, students have reported seeing Chauncey Morton's silhouette in Augustana's Andreen Hall. Noises have also been heard in connection with the sightings.

According to Swanson, it is not known if racism was part of the incident. "The student was eventually convicted of involuntary manslaughter," he said. "Was Chauncey's death intentional, or was it the result of a game that went too far? We'll probably never know for sure."

IGOR'S BISTRO

There are several haunted restaurants around the country, including Muriel's in New Orleans, Louisiana; Casey Moore's Oyster House in Tempe, Arizona; Earnestine & Hazel's in Memphis, Tennessee; the Fenton Hotel Tavern & Grill in Fenton, Michigan; and Foredough's Restaurant in Minneapolis.

Is there one in the Quad Cities?

You betcha. Do you love vintage Universal movies featuring vampires, mummies and Frankenstein's monster? Do you eagerly await Halloween every year and visit all the local homes decorated for trick-or-treaters? And most importantly, do you enjoy a hearty meal?

If you said *yes* to all the questions above, then you ought to visit Igor's Bistro, a Halloween-themed restaurant that's open all year. It's located at 3055 Thirty-Eighth Street, next to the Saukie Golf Course in Rock Island, Illinois. It's a favorite venue of locals and a fun, memorable dining venue for out-of-towners.

Igor's Bistro also enjoys the distinction of being haunted.

Co-owner and chef Rick Lopez left his job in the construction industry after twenty-five years to start the restaurant. "The construction industry was giving me way too much stress, and I felt that it was time to go back to what really makes me happy…cooking and all things creepy," he said.

The walls of Igor's Bistro are decked in horror movie and Halloween memorabilia, including posters from *Frankenstein*, *The Creature from the Black Lagoon* and *The Mummy*. You'll also find Mexican Day of the Dead skulls,

The sign for Igor's Bistro, a year-round Halloween-themed restaurant located at 3055 Thirty-Eighth Street, Rock Island. The one-hundred-plus-year-old building is home to a spirit named Toby. *Photo by Michael McCarty.*

zombie warnings, fake skeletons, gargoyle décor and a reproduction of the October 27, 1945 cover of *The New Yorker* by Edna Eicke and a poster of the story of Stingy Jack that Lopez penned himself. Stingy Jack is a mythical/folklore character associated with Halloween and the history of the jack-o'-lantern.

Entrees that are served at the bistro include Bat Wings (also known as chicken wings), Vampire Bites (mini salted pretzels in spicy cheese sauce), the Gremlin (a robust beef sandwich) and the Reubenstein (a unique take on a corned beef sandwich), among others.

Built in the early 1900s, this former residence has passed through several hands—from home to insurance company office, to florist and gift shop, to Ganson's Restaurant and now Igor's Bistro, which opened in April 2017. And somewhere along the way, the building has apparently picked up some eerie spirits. Lopez said:

> *When we first opened, the Illinois Paranormal Research Group came here to check the place out, to see if we were haunted or not. It ended with inconclusive results. But about a year later, they came back again and did another investigation. This time, they did indeed confirm that the ghosts of as many as five deceased spirits linger on the first three floors of the restaurant.*

Lopez added that the spirits make their presence known.

> *The ghost in the waitress station likes to cause trouble by changing music settings, knocking pictures off the walls, and tossing wine glasses and*

ketchup bottles at the servers. One night my wife, Kathy, was the last person out of the building and when I opened the next morning, there was a gallon jug of pancake syrup sitting in the middle of the floor. Now, I know she would not have left a jug of syrup in the middle of the floor like that.

There have been other strange and unusual occurrences, too. "Over the last year and a half, there have been many accounts of a young boy, about age ten to fourteen, appearing in the background of the old mirror that hangs in the bathroom hall," Lopez said. "Also, pans have hit the floor by themselves, and faucets have turned on when no one is in the kitchen."

The staff at Igor's Bistro have affectionately named the boy specter Toby. "Undoubtedly, Toby was responsible for the maple syrup incident," Lopez stated.

There have been reports of other spirits at the restaurant as well, Lopez stated.

There are two spirits that hang out in the dining room and like to play around with some of our more spiritually sensitive guests. During our one-year anniversary, we had colorful balloons at each table and a guest came up to me after the celebration. She said that a ghostly child touched her hair and whispered, "Tell them I like the blue ones." Now that was creepy because she had never been here before.

Lopez noted that another ghost lives in the basement and wants to be left alone.

One night, during a busy dinner rush, the Coke went out in the soda fountain and the dishwasher was too scared to go downstairs and change it. She eventually obliged and went down. When she got to the soda boxes, all the plastic syrup bags were pulled out of their boxes. She pushed all of them back in and went to grab a new box. When she turned back around to the rack, all the plastic bags were back out of their boxes. After that, the dishwasher quit.

Lopez told of another ghost in the bistro with a gentler disposition.

Sometimes late at night, when we are closed, we hear the very soft patter of feet walking in the dining room and detect the scent of lavender. We feel this is the spirit of a young girl. With all the strange goings-on and unexplained happenings, we believe that Toby and the others are making it known that it is still their home, too.

If that's the case, no doubt Toby and his spectral friends all must appreciate the macabre decorations in the restaurant. "Come visit Igor's Bistro, a local haunt," Lopez said with a laugh. "Take a selfie or two, and who knows! You might catch an unexplained orb or two, or some other creepy phenomenon."

ROCK ISLAND ARSENAL

The Rock Island Arsenal is located on 946 acres of land on Arsenal Island, originally known as Rock Island, on the Mississippi River. The island is located between the cities of Davenport, Iowa, and Rock Island, Illinois. It is the home of First Army headquarters, which, according to its Facebook page, "advises, assists, trains, mobilizes, deploys, redeploys and demobilizes Reserve Component forces." The island was established as a government site in 1816 with the building of Fort Armstrong. According to Wikipedia, the Rock Island Arsenal is the largest government-owned weapons manufacturing arsenal in the United States.

Wikipedia also reveals that on May 6, 1856, the steamer *Effie Afton* collided with the Arsenal Bridge. The bridge was damaged, while the steamer caught fire and sank. Fortunately, the crew was rescued. Steamboat companies demanded that the bridge be dismantled, and they sued to lend weight to their argument. Abraham Lincoln, who was a lawyer at the time, was hired by the M&M and Rock Island Line to defend the bridge. Eventually, the case went before the Supreme Court. The case, which ended in a hung jury, was dismissed, but after another suit in 1862, it was determined that the bridge would remain standing.

After Abraham Lincoln became president, he signed a bill to establish national arsenals at Columbus, Ohio; Indianapolis, Indiana; and Rock Island, Illinois.

In his autobiography, Chief Black Hawk commented on the presence of a fort on the island: "When we arrived we found that the troops had come to

Quarters One is the home of the highest-ranking office on the Rock Island Arsenal, located on Arsenal Island, Rock Island. This is the second-largest federally owned residence, the first being the White House. *Historic American Buildings Survey, Creator, and Thomas Jefferson Rodman. Rock Island Arsenal, Building No. 1, Gillespie Avenue between Terrace Drive & Hedge Lane, Rock Island, Rock Island County, IL. Illinois Rock Island Rock Island County, 1933. Documentation Compiled After. Photograph. https://www.loc.gov/item/il0528.*

Rock Island Arsenal Bridge. *Library of Congress; Rothstein, Arthur, photographer. Bridge across Mississippi, Davenport, Iowa. United States, 1940. Feb. Photograph. https://www.loc.gov/item/2017726853.*

The Government Bridge, also known as the Arsenal Bridge, spans the Mississippi River between Rock Island and Davenport and is adjacent to Mississippi River Lock & Dam No. 15. *Photo by Raymond Congrove.*

build a fort on Rock Island," he wrote. "We did not object, however, to their building their fort on the island, but were very sorry, as this was the best one on the Mississippi, and had long been the resort of our young people during the summer."

Located by the southeast corner of Arsenal Island, the Rock Island Confederate Cemetery is a remnant of a huge prison camp that once held thousands of Confederate soldiers. Nearly two thousand prisoners of war, victims of smallpox and pneumonia, are buried in the cemetery.

In Margaret Mitchell's classic novel *Gone with the Wind*, Ashley Wilkes was said to be imprisoned at Rock Island, where "three-fourths of all the men sent there never came out alive." The figures quoted in the book were inaccurate and were not used in the movie.

COLONEL DAVENPORT HOME

In 1783, Colonel George Davenport was born in Lincolnshire, England. Wikipedia described him as

> [a] *sailor, frontiersman, fur trader, merchant, postmaster, US Army soldier, Indian agent, and city planner. A prominent and well-known settler in the Iowa Territory, he was one of the earliest settlers in Rock Island, Illinois. He spent much of his life involved in the early settlement of the Mississippi Valley and the Quad Cities. The present-day city of Davenport, Iowa, is named after him.*

Davenport came to America in 1804. In 1816, he began work as a sutler, providing supplies for Fort Armstrong's troops. In time he became a fur trader. In 1833, Davenport built a house on what is now the Rock Island Arsenal. There he hosted meetings where plans for the future of the area were determined. The Davenport House came to be known as "the cradle of the Quad Cities."

John Brassard Jr. had this to say about Colonel George Davenport:

> *He was a very wealthy man and had one of the first finest homes built in the Quad Cities. He was rumored to have a bunch of money and gold in a safe in his house. A gang of outlaws known as the Prairie Bandits, seven individuals I believe, robbed and beat him, and he finally relented. They got into the safe and there were only six-hundred dollars inside.*

"[It was] regarded as one of the most infamous murders in the region," noted Kyle Dickson. "Independence Day turned into a nightmare for one of the city's most well respected and namesake. This tragedy is still remembered along with the efforts of the community members to find justice."

According to Brassard, Davenport—who was in his sixties—was beaten badly by the bandits. Fortunately, two fishermen, a father and son, heard his cries for help. They fetched a doctor and provided him with medical attention. In time, Davenport could identify the attackers.

"If memory serves me correctly," Brassard said, "they caught all seven and hung them all, one of them twice because the rope broke. Normally, that would have been okay and they would have let him be free, because he survived the hanging. But that wasn't okay with them. They made sure the job was done with the second hanging."

Brassard noted that he heard that Colonel Davenport eventually died in his home, but "I've never heard of any ghost stories associated with him there." Originally, he was buried a few feet from his home. His gravesite was later moved to Chippiannock Cemetery in Rock Island.

Over the years, the *Rock Island Argus* and *Moline Dispatch* have sponsored local ghost stories to be read at the Colonel Davenport house around Halloween.

Quarters One

"A rsenal Island has a long history, including housing prisoners of war during the Civil War," said Kyle Dickson. "It also produced infantry equipment for the Spanish American War."

Dickson stated that he did research on the arsenal when he was in college. Also, he knows George Eaton, a historian, who wrote the book *Rock Island Arsenal*. "He gave us a tour of the mansion, Quarters One, on the island," he said. "The home of the highest-ranking office on the Rock Island Arsenal and the second largest federal owned resident second only to the White House. It is a really grand estate, done in the Romanesque Revival style."

He noted that lots of ghost stories are associated with Quarters One. "Many people see prisoners of war," he said. "There was a lot of sickness that ran through the POW camps. It ran rampant. Reportedly, people see a lot of Confederate soldiers, especially in the entrances."

He observed that the cast iron used to build Quarters One came from reclaimed cannon balls, taken from battle. "The iron was melted down to create the lattice structure around the porch," he said. "The building is from the iron and steel of cannon balls, bayonets, stuff like that—all melted down."

Dickson added:

> *Brevet Brigadier General Thomas J. Rodman, who is called "The Father of the Rock Island Arsenal," never lived at Quarters One, but did have his funeral held in the parlor there. It was the first major gathering at the*

mansion. There have been a few stories about people possibly dying there. There is a rumor of a suicide in the house.

I've heard that the basement level was used as a hospital/training center for a little bit during World War I. I've also heard it was used as a makeshift courthouse for some reason, I am not 100 percent sure of the validity of those stories. I do know there is a room called the Charles Lindbergh Room.

Lindbergh visited the area in 1927 while touring the country after his famous solo flight across the Atlantic Ocean. "Lindbergh was invited to stay at the arsenal by the colonel himself," Dickson said. "There was a parade for Lindbergh, followed by a banquet for him."

Other dignitaries who have stayed at Quarters One include King Carl XVI Gustaf and Queen Silvia of Sweden in 1996. They also visited Augustana College.

"The Lindbergh Room at Quarters One is reportedly haunted," Dickson said.

That is where he stayed. Nobody says the ghost is Lindbergh. But people will say they see faces in the windows all the time. People underneath that floor will hear boot steps above them, pretty frequently.

Then there is the Pink Room, which is adjacent to the Lindbergh Room, connected by a bathroom. Apparently, people's food gets thrown around in that room. On more than one instance, someone's clothes were taken out of their suitcases and folded up and piled along the wall. People have smelled cinnamon and roses in that room.

Dickson said there have been a lot of odd happenings at Quarters One. "There are the servant's quarters and the butler's room," he said.

People see ghosts sliding down the banisters. They think it might have been the maids. They were known to do that, behind people's backs. The clock in the doorway is original to the house. People frequently see faces looking at them through the reflection. George Eaton was there when all the windows on the second floor opened simultaneously.

The Rock Island Paranormal team has investigated Quarters One off and on, from 2008 to 2018.

According to team member Ariel Young, "We were the first paranormal team to do so, too." She listed some of the paranormal activities they have experienced:

> We have had people get scratched, we've had people get pushed. We had a possession at one point—that one actually was caught on videotape, it was one of our own members. He fell asleep on the second floor, he was lying in the Lindbergh Room. All this happened in the Blue Room. We actually had a lot more activity in the Blue Room and in the basement, than throughout the whole house.

Surrounding Quad Cities Area

MILAN, ILLINOIS

VANDRUFF ISLAND

Vandruff Island is located in the Rock River, south of the city of Rock Island, Illinois, and north of Milan. The island is mostly composed of a quarry, and the west side features some residential development. It is also in the area of the Hennepin Canal (see Augustana College chapter for more details).

A few years ago, Moline resident Joan Vargas experienced a paranormal encounter on Vandruff Island. "I was fishing on the Rock River with my ex," she said, "and I saw this Indian warrior standing by him. I said, 'Honey, there's an Indian brave behind you.' He was wearing a full headdress or war bonnet." According to Vargas, her ex did not believe her, so he ignored her and kept on fishing.

"A few days later," Vargas said, "we were watching the local news and there was a story about a little boy who fell into the Rock River, exactly where we were fishing. The kid said he was saved by an Indian who lifted him out of the river, and then disappeared."

Vandruff Island has a history with Native Americans. In her book *Pathway to the Present in 50 Iowa and Illinois Communities*, Julie Jensen McDonald notes:

> *In 1828, Rinnah Wells came to the present Milan, Illinois, area and built his cabin on the north side of the Rock River. Joshua Vandruff arrived*

The Steel Dam at the Hennepin Canal on Vandruff Island on the Rock River, Milan. The Hennepin was the first American canal built of concrete without stone-cut facings. The engineering innovations used to build it were a bonus to the construction industry. The canal was used as a training ground for engineers who later worked on the Panama Canal. *Photo by Michael McCarty.*

in 1829, building a home near the later site of the Sears Mill until he completed his house on the island named after him.

These first settlers lived peaceably near a colony of Kickapoo Indians on the south shore of the Rock River and Black Hawk's village, Saukenuk, was across the river.

Many times, ghosts are considered to be dangerous, malevolent entities. But really, why should a ghost have to be evil? Doesn't it make more sense to think that good people become good spirits after they die? It is awe-inspiring to learn that a ghost of the Quad-Cities could have saved a little boy's life.

MONMOUTH, ILLINOIS

CRYBABY BRIDGE

In autumn, the picturesque countryside surrounding Monmouth, Illinois, is reminiscent of the fields and winding roads you'll see in the classic horror movie *Night of the Living Dead*. And like that fictional rural setting, the gravel lanes of Monmouth hold a disturbing secret. At the address of 2309–11 Sixtieth Street in Monmouth, you'll find the Crybaby Bridge, and it is the home of ghostly secrets.

The Crybaby Bridge in Monmouth isn't the only haunted bridge with that nickname in America. Crybaby Bridges can be found in Maryland, Ohio, Oklahoma, South Carolina, Texas, Utah and Virginia. Some states even have multiple Crybaby Bridges.

In most cases, the bridge in question received that name because the sound of crying infants can be heard from the bridge. Often there is an urban legend attached to the area that concerns children in peril. Some legends state that babies met their deaths near the bridges, and the ghosts of the mothers may also haunt the locales near the bridges. Also, it is often said that supernatural occurrences may transpire if you park on one of the Crybaby Bridges. Your vehicle may move if you park in neutral on the bridge.

Bridges in general have been the sites of countless personal tragedies around the world. Many times, people have committed suicide by jumping from bridges. Suicide bridges can be found around the world, from America

The graffiti-covered Crybaby Bridge in Monmouth. According to local legend, if you put baby powder on your bumper and shift your vehicle to neutral, a ghost will push the vehicle and leave fingerprints in the powder. *Photo by Michael McCarty.*

to Australia to South Africa and more. In many metropolitan communities, some bridges draw so many suicide attempts that physical barriers need to be erected to discourage future fatal incidents.

What do all these bridges have in common? They all have compelling, tragic tales as part of their histories, and the Crybaby Bridge in Monmouth is no exception. Kyle Dickson attended college in Monmouth and said that at the time he heard many tales of the bridge. The Crybaby Bridge is a small graffiti-covered structure with metal rails, crossing Cedar Creek on a hilly gravel road. The place has been a hot spot for urban legends for decades. The first, most commonly told story is that a bus full of children ran off the bridge, and many of them drowned. That claim seems dubious, since there do not appear to be signs of that sort of extensive damage to the bridge. Plus, the creek is extremely shallow. A person could walk across easily. So it is doubtful that anyone, even a child, could have drowned in such an accident.

He offered this information about how to experience supernatural phenomena on the Monmouth bridge. "Go to the bridge, turn off your car

A black toy rat left at the Crybaby Bridge. *Photo by Michael McCarty.*

and put it in neutral, and your car seemingly gets pushed across the bridge," he said. "You're supposed to sprinkle baby powder on the back of your car and small handprints will form on the bumpers and rear window."

Dickson added that this phenomena is linked with claims that children died on the bridge. "The spirits of the kids don't want you to suffer the same fate, so they will push you across the bridge. At the end, the windows are supposed to fog up and you'll see a bunch of hand prints."

According to Dickson, there is also a story about a woman and child in a horse-drawn carriage. "For some reason, a wheel fell off, or there was some kind of an accident and her child died," he said. "At the Crybaby Bridge, you hear the crying of a baby late at night. Sometimes you hear the cry of a banshee—the mother screaming for her lost child. There is another variation of the same story that says the mother's baby died and she's looking for it. Or, the mother committed suicide on the bridge because her child died."

Yet a third story states that a farmer went insane and drowned his child in the water. None of these tales has been reported or archived in any of the local newspapers or libraries. Plus, any legend about the bridge that says someone drowned in the creek does not take into account the shallow level of the water. To be fair, it is possible that the creek's water level may have been higher in past years during periods of heavier rainfall.

The narrow iron bridge has been the site of several paranormal investigations, séances, local newspaper and radio fodder and many videos on YouTube. People have reported seeing strange images in photographs taken at the bridge, or hearing strange voices on recordings, even though no one else was around.

In early November 2018, authors Mark McLaughlin and Michael McCarty drove to the Crybaby Bridge in Monmouth to see what they might find.

McCarty commented:

> *The desolate location gave the structure an unnerving atmosphere. What makes this location even more eerie is the fact that there are so many other Crybaby Bridges across the country. It makes you wonder if each bridge is part of some greater supernatural mystery. It's almost as though these metal bridges draw spiritual energy to them, like magnets.*

McLaughlin added:

> *The minute you see the Crybaby Bridge, you realize that something out of the ordinary is going on. When we arrived, we immediately noticed that the bridge was covered with multi-colored graffiti. And the thing is, the bridge is small and quite remote, practically lost in its rural setting—why would anyone drive that distance just to spray-paint a bridge? While we were there, another vehicle stopped on the bridge, and the passenger parked on the bridge and got out to look at it.*

McCarty and McLaughlin saw that some previous visitor had placed a large plastic black rat on the bridge's railing. They also noticed some beer cans at different points around the bridge, and even some men's underwear near the water. Apparently, people come to the bridge to party every now and then. For better or worse, people are compelled to visit the bridge.

As stated earlier, it is believed that on many of the Crybaby Bridges, haunting spirits will move your vehicle, if you park on the bridge. So, McCarty and McLaughlin decided to put that notion to the test.

They did several experiments, putting the car in neutral on both sides of the bridge. Sure enough, it felt like it was being pushed, like the story goes. At one point, McCarty placed his vehicle in neutral in the middle of the bridge facing southeast. The vehicle slowly began to creep toward the southeastern end.

He then placed the vehicle in neutral in the middle facing northwest, and the vehicle slowly moved backward toward the southeastern end.

"When I put the car in neutral in the middle of the bridge," McCarty said, "it wouldn't move. That could be because it was the most even spot in the bridge."

Before they'd made their parking tests, they had sprinkled talcum powder on the front and back fenders. But at no point did any handprints or other disruptions of the powder appear.

"A skeptic might say that the vehicle moved because of gravity," McLaughlin said. "But, when it did move, it began to roll fairly quickly. For the vehicle to roll that quickly, one would have expected more of an incline to the road."

Dickson offered this explanation about the movement of vehicles on the bridge. "The way the hill is situated, it looks like it is straight," he said, "but instead, gravity still pushes you down."

He compared the Crybaby Bridge to the Mystery House at the Calico Ghost Town in Yermo, California—a rustic, abandoned mining whistle-stop in the desert. "The Mystery House looks fine until you actually start moving around inside," he said. "The guy who built it had one leg shorter than the other. Also, because it is on a hill and gravity pushes downward, things that seem to go straight actually go the completely opposite way."

Did the visit prove beyond a shadow of a doubt that the bridge is haunted? No. But, it did result in an experience that was both disturbing and thought-provoking.

The Crybaby Bridge is clearly a compelling place for ghost hunters to visit. The space under the bridge seems vaguely threatening, and at night, the locale is downright disturbing. Both McCarty and McLaughlin agreed that there was something definitely a bit "off" about the bridge. Something not quite right.

"Mike and I spent at least a half hour on and around that bridge," McLaughlin said.

Looking back on the experience, I now realize that neither of us touched the black plastic rat on that bridge rail. If we'd been in a novelty shop, I certainly would have picked it up and looked at it, no problem. So why didn't I touch it? For that matter, why didn't I take it with me, as a souvenir of the visit? I'm not saying that the toy rat was evil or haunted. I think I didn't touch it because it wasn't my property. It belonged to the bridge.

McLaughlin also noted that bridges in general have special cultural significance.

Bridges have always represented life's transitions, including the final transition into death. Even in social media, you'll note that when people talk about a pet's death, they'll say that their furry friend has crossed the rainbow bridge. That symbolism is actually older than most people realize. In Norse mythology, Bifröst is the rainbow bridge that crosses from Midgard, the land of humanity, to Asgard, the world of the gods. We trust bridges to carry us safely to our destinations, and because we hope that all of our transitions will be successful, we use bridges to symbolize that hope.

BIBLIOGRAPHY

Books

Brassard, John, and John Brassard Jr. *Scott County Cemeteries*. Charleston, SC: Arcadia Publishing, 2011.

Brassard, John, Jr. *Murder and Mayhem in Scott County, Iowa*. Charleston, SC: The History Press, 2018.

Eaton, George. *Rock Island Arsenal*. Charleston, SC: Arcadia Publishing, 2014.

Hamer, Richard, and Roger Ruthhart. *Citadel of Sin: The John Looney Story*. Moline, IL: Moline Dispatch Publishing, 2007.

Highland Park Historical District History & Architecture. Rock Island, IL: City of Rock Island, 2004.

History & Architecture: Broadway Historic District. Rock Island, IL: City of Rock Island, 2007.

McDonald, Julie Jensen. *Pathways to the Present: 50 Iowa & Illinois Communities*. Davenport, IA: Boyar Books, 1977.

Powers-Douglas, Minda. *Chippiannock Cemetery*. Charleston, SC: Arcadia Publishing, 2010.

The Amazing Kreskin, and Michael McCarty. *Conversations with Kreskin*. West Caldwell, NJ: Team Kreskin Production LLC, 2012.

Trollinger, Vernon. *Haunted Iowa City*. Charleston, SC: Haunted America, 2011.

Turner, Jonathan. *A Brief History of Bucktown: Davenport's Infamous District Transformed*. Charleston, SC: The History Press, 2016.

Wood, Sharon E. *The Freedom of Streets: Work, Citizenship & Sexuality in a Golden Age City*. Chapel Hill: University of North Carolina Press, 2005.

Articles and Websites

Arpy, Jim. "A Ghost Chaser Unravels the Mystery of Davenport's 'Haunted House.'" *Quad-City Times*, May 11, 1972.

Booker, Roy. "Moline's Cemetery Black Angel Now in New Mexico." *Quad-City Times*, October 30, 2014.

Brassard, John, Jr. "Was the Phi Kappa Chi House One of the Most Haunted Houses in Davenport, Iowa?" Kitchen Table Historian. www.johnbrassardjr.com.

Hayden, Sarah. "Bump in the Night: Paranormal Team Investigates Hauntings." *Rock Island Argus/Moline Dispatch*, October 28, 2018.

Marx, John. "Demo Queen: Rock Island Woman Loves Tearing Down Buildings." *Rock Island Argus/Moline Dispatch*, December 22, 2018.

Oakdale Memorial Gardens. "History." https://www.oakdalememorialgardens.org/history.

Pokora, Richard. "Abbey Overlooks History of Downtown Bettendorf." *Quad-City Times*, September 9, 2015.

Richardson-Sloane Special Collections Center of the Davenport Public Library. "The Orphans of Oakdale Cemetery." October 13, 2008. https://blogs.davenportlibrary.com.

———. "Still Doing His Rounds: The Haunting of 723 Main Street." October 30, 2014. https://blogs.davenportlibrary.com.

Willard, John. "Moline's Black Angel Revisited." *Quad-City Times*, November 25, 2003.

Wundram, Bill. "The Bleak Cemetery of Forgotten Children." *Quad-City Times*, August 29, 1993.

About the Authors

Michael McCarty, Crybaby Bridge, fall 2018. *Photo by Cindy McCarty.*

Michael McCarty has been a professional writer since 1983 and the author of over forty books of fiction and nonfiction, including *I Kissed a Ghoul*, *A Little Help from My Fiends*, *Dark Duets*, *Liquid Diet & Midnight Snack*, *Monster behind the Wheel* (co-written with Mark McLaughlin), *Dracula Transformed and Other Bloodthirsty Tales* (also with Mark McLaughlin), *Lost Girl of the Lake* (with Joe McKinney), *Ghostly Tales of Route 66* (co-written with Connie Corcoran Wilson), the vampire *Bloodless* series: *Bloodless*, *Bloodlust* and *Bloodline* (co-written with Jody LaGreca). He is a five-time Bram Stoker Finalist and in 2008 won the David R. Collins' Literary Achievement Award from the Midwest Writing Center.

He is also the author of the mega-book of interviews *Modern Mythmakers: 35 Interviews with Horror and Science Fiction Writers and Filmmakers*, which features interviews with Ray Bradbury, Dean Koontz, John Carpenter, Richard Matheson, Elvira, Linnea Quigley, John Saul, Joe McKinney and many more. His latest book is *Dark Cities: Dark Tales*, a collection of solo and collaborative horror tales.

Michael McCarty lives in Rock Island, Illinois, with his wife, Cindy, and pet rabbit Latte.

Michael McCarty is on Twitter as michaelmccarty6.

His blog site is at: http://monstermikeyaauthor.wordpress.com.

Like him on his official Facebook page: http://www.facebook.com/michaelmccarty.horror. You can also snail mail him at:

Michael McCarty
Fan Mail
P.O. Box 4441
Rock Island, IL 61204-4441

MARK MCLAUGHLIN is a Bram Stoker Award–winning author of fiction, nonfiction and poetry. His writings have appeared in more than one thousand magazines, newspapers, websites and anthologies, including *Galaxy*, *Living Dead 2*, *Writer's Digest*, *Cemetery Dance*, *Midnight Premiere*, *Dark Arts* and two volumes of *Year's Best Horror Stories* (DAW Books).

Mark McLaughlin at the Crybaby Bridge, fall 2018. *Photo by Michael McCarty.*

Mark's latest paperback releases are the Lovecraftian story collections *Horrors & Abominations: 24 Tales of the Cthulhu Mythos* and *The House of the Ocelot & More Lovecraftian Nightmares*, both coauthored by Michael Sheehan Jr.

Other collections of Mark's fiction include *Hideous Faces, Beautiful Skulls*; *Best Little Witch-House in Arkham*; *Beach Blanket Zombie*; and the two-author vampire collection with Michael McCarty, *Dracula Transformed & Other Bloodthirsty Tales*. Mark and Michael McCarty have also co-written the horror novel *Monster behind the Wheel*.

Mark's latest Kindle release is *The Idol in the Hedge Maze: A Lovecraftian Novelette*, coauthored by Michael Sheehan Jr. Mark McLaughlin is also the coauthor, with Rain Graves and David Niall Wilson, of *The Gossamer Eye*, a paperback poetry collection that won the 2002 Bram Stoker Award for Superior Achievement in Poetry.

Additional Kindle releases by Mark include the fiction collections *Magic Cannot Die*, *Foreign Tongue* and *Drunk on the Wine that Pours from My Wicked Eyes*. With Michael Sheehan Jr., Mark has written a series of Lovecraftian Kindle collections: *Stainless Steel Sarcophagus*, *The Testament of Cthulhu*, *The Creature in the Waxworks*, *The Relic in the Egyptian Gallery*, *Shoggoth Apocalypse*, *The Blasphemy in the Canopic Jar*, *The Horror in the Water Tower* and *The Abominations of Nephren-Ka*.

For more information on Mark McLaughlin's books, visit BMovieMonster.com. You can also find Mark and his books on Amazon.com.